YOU HAVE THE ADVANTAGE

Harrison House

Shippensburg, PA

YOU HAVE THE ADVANTAGE

WALKING IN THE REVELATION OF GOD'S COVENANT OF BLESSING, FAVOR, AND STRENGTH

BARRY BENNETT

© Copyright 2024 — Barry Bennett

Printed in the United States of America. All rights reserved. No portion of this book may be reproduced, stored in a retrieval system, or transmitted in any form or by any means—electronic, mechanical, photocopy, recording, scanning, or other—except for brief quotations in critical reviews or articles, without the prior written permission of the publisher. Unless otherwise identified, Scripture quotations are taken from the New King James Version. Copyright © 1982 by Thomas Nelson, Inc. Used by permission. All rights reserved.

Scripture quotations marked NASB are taken from the NEW AMERICAN STANDARD BIBLE®, Copyright © 1960, 1962, 1963, 1968, 1971, 1972, 1973, 1975, 1977, 1995 by The Lockman Foundation. Used by permission.

Scripture quotations marked KJV are taken from the King James Version. All emphasis within Scripture quotations is the author's own.

CONTENTS

Foreword by Andrew Wommack 7

You Have the Advantage!. 8

Chapter 1   Born Again! 11

Chapter 2   The Power of God 17

Chapter 3   A New Kingdom 22

Chapter 4   A New Language. 26

Chapter 5   You Have Life-Changing Power! 31

Chapter 6   What Do You See? 40

Chapter 7   Your Perception of Yourself. 47

Chapter 8   Your Perception of Circumstances. 50

Chapter 9   The Advantage of Freedom 53

Chapter 10   The Blessing 56

Chapter 11   Favor with God! 67

Chapter 12   You Can Hear God! 76

Chapter 13   Fellowship with God 84

Chapter 14   The Advantage of Peace with God.......90

Chapter 15   The Advantage of an Image 97

Chapter 16   The Advantage of Joy 104

Chapter 17   The Advantage of Thankfulness 107

Chapter 18   The Advantage of Faith. 114

Chapter 19   The Advantage of Unbelief 123

Chapter 20   So Many Advantages! 127

Chapter 21   You Always Have the Advantage
              in Christ............................... 136

              About Barry Bennett................... 139

FOREWORD

B arry Bennett has been a Godsend to me and Charis Bible College. After having a successful ministry in Chile and directing a Spanish-speaking Bible College back in the States, he came to us simply at the leading of the Lord. He answered mail for us for two years without promoting himself before we discovered what an awesome minister he was. He is consistently one of our students' favorite instructors.

I've seen him battle through cancer and come out victorious. He truly loves the Lord and has an anointing to share deep truths he has learned in a very simple way. Barry has been a tremendous blessing to me, and I know this book will be a blessing to you. We truly have the advantage through our Lord Jesus Christ.

Andrew Wommack
President and Founder of Andrew Wommack Ministries
and Charis Bible College

YOU HAVE THE ADVANTAGE!

There was a commercial on TV about some kids picking teams for a basketball game. The kids were around 10 years old, but one of the potential players was a Hall of Fame basketball player who seemed gigantic next to the children. He was picked for a team, and that team instantly had the advantage. There was no way they could lose with such a powerful presence on the team.

In the story of David and Goliath, the situation was reversed. Goliath was the imposing force who was seemingly invincible. His opponent was a young man with a slingshot and some rocks. This battle looked to be over before it even began. However, the young David was aware of his covenant as a child of the nation of Israel. He recognized that his opponent had no covenant with God. Regardless of his size, strength, and mighty weapon, he was no match for a young man who recognized his advantage. David killed the giant with a slingshot and won a great victory for Israel. In this case, it wasn't the physical attributes of either fighter that made the difference. It was the knowledge that David had of the faithfulness of God. With God on his side, David knew he could not lose.

My people are destroyed for lack of knowledge (Hosea 4:6).

As born-again believers in Jesus Christ, we have entered into a covenant of blessings, favor, and strength that is more powerful than most of us have imagined. We have the advantage in life, but sadly most are not aware of the greatness of this covenant. In fact, many religious teachings teach against the promises of the covenant and focus on suffering and fatalism in this life. Though believers have the advantage, they often don't know it or don't believe it.

Many are burdened with the challenges of life to the point of feeling they have no hope. Some have become so immersed in their feelings of discouragement that they question whether God cares at all. The advantages of His presence in our lives are ignored or not understood.

The purpose of this book is to awaken you to the incredible advantages you, the believer, have for living an abundant, overcoming life. You have been blessed with all blessings and equipped with the presence of God in your life. You have been re-created to *"reign in life"* (Romans 5:17)! Will you believe and apply your advantages?

CHAPTER 1

BORN AGAIN!

Much of Christian teaching is focused on survival rather than victory. We have been shaped by Christian culture to believe that we are basically helpless in the face of the circumstances of the world. In fact, many believe that the circumstances are being managed, and even micro-managed, by God Himself. The Christian is oftentimes expected to believe that he or she is helpless in the face of sickness, poverty, and tragedy. We are exhorted to "hang on" and understand that "God is in control." If you believe that, fatalism is being subtly encouraged, and "faith" is many times redefined as fate.

Such teaching not only misrepresents the gospel but creates a class of unbelieving believers who only gather together to console each other in their ongoing losses in life. And we wonder why millions are staying away from the church! The advantages of the gospel are often not understood.

What happened at the new birth?

When you first believed in the Lord, some things took place that you probably weren't fully aware of. Let's look at some of what transpired.

You passed from death to life!

> *Most assuredly, I say to you, he who hears My word and believes in Him who sent Me has everlasting life, and shall not come into judgment, but has passed from death into life* (John 5:24).

If that is not an advantage, I don't know what is! While the unbelievers around us are alive physically, they are not alive in the spiritual sense of the word. When we believe the Word of God and the revelation of Jesus dying and rising again for us, we are born again, recreated, and our spirits are made alive to God. Believers are the only people on this earth who are truly alive!

YOU ARE A NEW CREATION!

> *Therefore, if anyone is in Christ, he is a new creation; old things have passed away; behold, all things have become new* (2 Corinthians 5:17).

What has become new? What has passed away?

> *Knowing this, that our old man was crucified with Him, that the body of sin might be done away with, that we should no longer be slaves of sin* (Romans 6:6).

The "old man" was a slave to sin, lust, fear, worry, and depression. Who has the advantage, the slave of sin or the "new creation" in Christ? The slave of sin who is still abiding in spiritual death (independence from God) is certainly at a disadvantage. Life must be navigated on the superficial level of circumstances, force of personality, genetic strengths or weaknesses, and educational opportunities. Even if all those factors add up in their favor, they are still "dead" and a slave to sin. There will be the continual struggle with guilt, lust, bitterness, offense, carnal ambition, rejection, fear, and depression. The list could go on and on. The outward façade of a successful life is actually quite hollow. Just a glance at the "rich and famous" of our day will reveal the emptiness that many experience.

YOU HAVE GOD INSIDE!

The born-again believer has God living in them! I'm not sure that many of us have fully grasped what this means. The potential of this "new creation" can't be overstated.

> *Jesus answered and said to him, "If anyone loves Me, he will keep My word; and My Father will love him, and We will come to him and make Our home with him"* (John 14:23).

The reality of the Father and the Son making their home in us is staggering. Is this not an advantage in life?

> *But he who is joined to the Lord is one spirit with Him* (1 Corinthians 6:17).

*Now we can understand that the Trinity of God actually lives within the believer. If you have the Spirit of God within, you are **never** at a disadvantage in life. You are alive from the dead and new within.*

The new birth experience not only gives life to our human spirit, which was cut off from God, it also makes our spirit "new." The word *new* means "recently made, fresh, recent, unused, unworn; of a new kind, unprecedented, novel, uncommon, unheard of."

Something that is new only holds promise for the future. It has no past. As a new creation in Christ, your past has been forgiven, washed away, and forgotten!

For I will be merciful to their unrighteousness, and their sins and their lawless deeds I will remember no more (Hebrews 8:12).

This incredible, transforming work of the Spirit happens when one's heart believes in the gospel of His grace. A new spiritual creation comes into being. Most believers understand this concept, but what we may not understand is that our "new man" never grows old. It gets renewed daily.

Therefore we do not lose heart. Even though our outward man is perishing, yet the inward man is being renewed day by day (2 Corinthians 4:16).

The word *renewed* means "to receive new strength and vigor; to be changed into a new kind of life as opposed to the former corrupt state." I didn't just get made new 50 years ago (at this writing) when I believed in Jesus. I am renewed daily! In fact, we can assume that our spirit man is receiving new strength and vigor moment by moment.

Nothing about God ever grows old; therefore, His Spirit in us is continually new. His grace does not wear out or diminish. His purpose for us never dies. His gifts in us are always available. His mercies are new every morning. Every day is literally a *new day* with a *new* life inside! Our minds are being transformed to comprehend this truth, and we grow in knowledge and wisdom, but our spirit man never grows old.

Today is a new beginning. If you need a new beginning, take it. Your spirit is receiving new strength and vigor right now, and now, and now, and now. You have the advantage! Don't languish in guilt, doubt, and self-condemnation. Don't be a slave to the emotions and lusts of the past. You are born again, alive from the dead, and one spirit with Him. Don't waste your advantage!

> Father, I declare my faith in the death, burial,
> and resurrection of Jesus Christ on my behalf.
> My sins are forgiven, and I am a new creation
> in Christ! I have newness of life, and You now
> live in me! Thank You for Your love and grace!

CHAPTER 2

THE POWER OF GOD

I was born again in the fall of 1972, and one of the "hot topics" of the time was the baptism in the Holy Spirit. It was very controversial, and apparently is still controversial in some circles today. Sadly, for many the subject is taboo, criticized, and even called heretical by some. Nevertheless, millions of believers continue to experience the outpouring of God's Spirit in their lives subsequent to their born-again experience. This happened to me in the spring of 1974.

I was studying this subject with my college roommate for a period of time and we made a list of arguments "for and against" the baptism in the Spirit. If there was more that God wanted me to have, I wanted it!

One night while praying over this, I was reading the gospel of Luke and came to this verse:

> *If you then, being evil, know how to give good*
> *gifts to your children, how much more will your*

*heavenly Father give the Holy Spirit to those who
ask Him!* (Luke 11:13)

Instantly I realized that this wasn't about me being good
enough, or holy enough, or worthy. I was righteous by the
grace of God, and His heart as a Father wanted to bless me.
With no "faith teaching" in my life at all, I simply knew
that if I asked for the Holy Spirit, God would honor His
Word.

I asked to receive, and nothing tangible happened. But
I chose to believe the Word and I began to thank God for
the power of the Holy Spirit in my life. I continued to
thank God the rest of the evening and into the next day. I
went to work praising God and came home thanking God.
I was filled with thankfulness by faith. I knew God cannot
lie. That evening, 24 hours after asking and believing, I was
again in my room praying and giving thanks. Suddenly I
moved from English to a heavenly language. It was a flood
of new words that I could speak from my spirit. I could
start, stop, get loud, or get soft. I was speaking, but the
Spirit was giving me the utterance in a heavenly language.
What a blessing!

That moment was the beginning of one of the greatest
advantages possible—to be endued with power from on
high.

Behold, I send the Promise of My Father upon you;
but tarry in the city of Jerusalem until you are
endued with power from on high (Luke 24:49).

As I began to understand, the gifts of the Holy Spirit were now available to me as never before. The gifts are tools for effective ministry. They are an outflow of love and compassion that can bring blessings to those in need.

The ability to communicate with God beyond my own finite mind and language opened up to me an advantage in the world of the Spirit that cannot be measured. My prayers in English would always be limited to what I think I know, but my prayers in the language of the Spirit were limited to what God knows, and God knows all!

I could now pray from the mind of Christ and be led by the Spirit as never before. I could now "see" the possibilities around me, the needs of others, and have access to the answers they needed. I had a divine advantage for life!

I don't have to get depressed, nervous, worried, or fearful. I can pray in the Spirit and build myself up in the Lord.

But you, beloved, building yourselves up on your
most holy faith, praying in the Holy Spirit (Jude
1:20).

I don't have to feel limited in my own strength and knowledge. The Spirit is upon me and in me for the purpose of victory. How does Paul describe this advantage?

> *Now may the God of hope fill you with all joy and peace in believing, that you may abound in hope **by the power of the Holy Spirit*** (Romans 15:13).

> *And my speech and my preaching were not with persuasive words of human wisdom, **but in demonstration of the Spirit and of power*** (1 Corinthians 2:4).

When you receive the gift of the Holy Spirit, you have an incredible advantage in life. You become a carrier of life and blessings to others. You are not limited to your human thoughts and emotions. The power of God is available to you to bless others and see the "impossible" as possible. You have the power to be His witness.

> *But you shall receive power when the Holy Spirit has come upon you; and you shall be witnesses to Me* (Acts 1:8).

This advantage is in many ways the door to the storehouse of advantages that the Lord has prepared for us.

If you have not received the gift of the Holy Spirit with the ability to pray in a heavenly language, you can receive it now.

> Father, according to Your Word, You give the Holy Spirit to those who ask. I am asking to receive this power and this blessing now, in Jesus' Name. I believe I receive, and I thank You for Your grace and power to be an effective witness of Your gospel. Amen!

> *If you then, being evil, know how to give good gifts to your children, how much more will your heavenly Father give the Holy Spirit to those who ask Him!* (Luke 11:13)

CHAPTER 3

A NEW KINGDOM

With my wife and three children, we moved to Chile in 1989 to minister the gospel. We spent 12 years in that beautiful country and God blessed our ministry. However, our time there was not without challenges. The immediate challenge was the language. If we were going to be successful in Chile, we had to learn Spanish. We also had to learn a new culture, new customs, the laws of the land, a new style of driving, how to ride crowded busses and subways, and how to shop. So much was different for us.

In a very real sense, we had changed "kingdoms." If we were to have an advantage in our new country, we would need to learn the language, culture, and customs. Consider the apostle Paul's declaration concerning the spiritual location of believers.

> *He has delivered us from the power of darkness and*
> *conveyed us into the kingdom of the Son of His love*
> (Colossians 1:13).

When we were born again, we changed dominions. Without even knowing or understanding what happened, we were delivered from "*the power of darkness*" and transferred into "*the kingdom of the Son of His love.*"

In this book we will discover many of the advantages of this transition, but unless we realize that there *has been* a transition, we will lose our advantages. Many Christians seem to never grasp that they are citizens of the Kingdom of God. They don't learn the language of God. They don't learn the spiritual laws and principles that govern the Kingdom. Many simply continue to live their born-again life with the language, culture, and customs of the "power of darkness."

Is there an advantage in understanding the Kingdom of God? Absolutely!

> *But seek first the kingdom of God and His righteousness, and all these things shall be added to you* (Matthew 6:33).

The "things" Jesus referred to are spelled out in the preceding verses. He is speaking of the daily needs of life. Jesus stated that if we establish a new priority of understanding His Kingdom and how it works, and understand the power of the gift of righteousness (right standing with God), the things of life that we need will be added to us. The implication is that God desires to meet our needs and will do so if our hearts have the right priority. That's an advantage! Those who only seek things, status, and power won't have the blessing of God on their lives. So how does the Kingdom work?

> *And He said, "The kingdom of God is as if a man should scatter seed on the ground, and should sleep by night and rise by day, and the seed should sprout and grow, he himself does not know how. For the earth yields crops by itself: first the blade, then the head, after that the full grain in the head. But when the grain ripens, immediately he puts in the sickle, because the harvest has come"* (Mark 4:26-29).

In these few verses, Jesus unlocks an incredible revelation that can give the believer untold advantages in life! The Kingdom is a "seed" Kingdom. If you can understand the power of a seed, you can begin to enter into the advantages of the Kingdom! We are all sowing continually. Words, thoughts, actions, and resources are all seeds that are being squandered or used for Kingdom purposes. In my book *Shaping Your Future*, by this same publisher, I discuss this revelation in detail.

Being citizens of the Kingdom of God activates possibilities that don't exist for the unbeliever. While it is God's heart that no one perish and that all come to know Him, many will not. The hearts of many are against the things of God, and sadly, these same ones can make life hard for those of us who love God. But—we have the advantage! We understand the Kingdom and how it works. We live in a different dimension of spiritual understanding, vision, and faith.

CHAPTER 4

A NEW LANGUAGE

In any new job or skill, you will need to learn the "language" of that environment. Every business has its own terms and clichés. Musicians have a language, every sport has a language, and doctors have a language. Each generation of young people has new slang and creates new words. Words are given new meanings from generation to generation. If you are going to function successfully in these settings, you will need to learn the language. It may still be English, but it will be a new way of saying things.

The Kingdom of God has a new language. It is the language of faith, hope, and love. While the world speaks of fears, doubts, and worries, believers speak of the promises of God and the realities of the New Covenant. As a born-again Christian, you have the capacity to speak words of life and faith. You have an advantage that an unbeliever doesn't have. And the advantage of life-giving words cannot be overstated! Let's look at the reality of God and His Word.

In the beginning was the Word, and the Word was
with God, and the Word was God (John 1:1).

Not only is His Word "with" Him, but the Word *is*
God! The very nature, divinity, and infiniteness of God is
contained in His Word, which is Him! We could probably
spend the rest of our lives hoping to entirely comprehend
this, but let's move on and see how this relates to us on a
daily basis.

By the word of the Lord the heavens were made,
and all the host of them by the breath of His mouth
(Psalm 33:6).

In the beginning God spoke. Creation is the outcome of
God's words and is sustained by God's words.

Upholding all things by the word of His power
(Hebrews 1:3).

That which was invisible to the natural eye was visible
to the heart and mind of God. God saw that which He
purposed and declared it. By His Word, the visible, tangible
world and the universe came into being. In the same way,
that which is visible and tangible is being continually
sustained or upheld by His Word. How powerful is His

Word? If God's Word somehow vanished from reality, everything that exists, visible and invisible, would simply disappear. The very fact that the visible and invisible exist is proof that His Word is alive and active.

The first use of words was to create. The power of God was released through His words. "Light be!" ("Let there be light") are the first spoken words we have recorded in the Bible, and in Genesis 1 we see the power that God's words have. They create and sustain the universe and are responsible for bringing forth mankind in His very image!

> *Then God **said**, "Let Us make man in Our image, according to Our likeness"* (Genesis 1:26).

Being created in the image of God includes the capacity to speak words! God's words created and continue to sustain all that is. I doubt that most of us have considered the incredible privilege and blessing that we have in speaking. We are a "God class" of creation (in His image) with the ability to speak. How are we using words?

The language of God in the beginning empowered mankind to accomplish His purposes. Consider God's words to Adam and Eve.

Then God blessed them, and God said to them, "Be fruitful and multiply; fill the earth and subdue it; have dominion over the fish of the sea, over the birds of the air, and over every living thing that moves on the earth" (Genesis 1:28).

God's words gave mankind dominion over the earth and a purpose to fulfill. God spoke a blessing over Adam and Eve. This wasn't some simple expression of goodwill but an empowering to walk in the abundant provision of God for the purpose of reigning over the earth, subduing it, and filling it with sons and daughters. God's heart was to have a family that bore His image and fulfilled His desires—by using His words!

I say all of this to make clear, especially to born-again believers, that the ability to speak words is the most powerful advantage that we can imagine. God used words to create, bless, and empower mankind to fulfill God's purposes. How are you using your words?

When Jesus was praying in the garden shortly before His arrest and trial, He was telling the Father of what He had accomplished during His earthly mission. One thing stands out as significant for this discussion.

For I have given to them the words which You have given Me; and they have received them (John 17:8).

I have given them Your word (John 17:14).

I saw this many years ago and understood that Jesus was stating something profound and potentially life changing for those who believe. The most precious and powerful resource available to believers is God's Word and God's words. This advantage cannot be overstated.

God used His first words to create, and we are created in His image with the capacity to speak. Have we understood the tremendous advantage we have in this fallen world?

Death and life are in the power of the tongue, and those who love it will eat its fruit (Proverbs 18:21).

Are we using the capacity to speak words only to complain, criticize, curse, worry, slander, and doubt? Are we throwing away the most powerful advantage we have?

The language of the Kingdom is the language of love, faith, hope, and blessing. It is a language that unbelievers can't speak. The born-again believer can declare the words of God and know that the invisible world of the Spirit springs into action on their behalf. We have the advantage!

CHAPTER 5

YOU HAVE LIFE-CHANGING POWER!

The advantage of words in the mouth of a believer is worth our time to consider further. If we can understand how God uses words, we can begin to see the potential that we have as His sons and daughters, made in His image, and filled with His Spirit.

In the story of Abraham, Paul, the author of the book of Romans, refers to God's declaration over Abraham's life. If you are familiar with the story, Abraham's name had been Abram, but God, in order to accomplish His purpose, changed Abram's name to Abraham, because He declared, "I have made you a father of many nations."

> (As it is written, "I have made you a father of many nations") in the presence of Him whom he believed—God, who gives life to the dead and **calls those things which do not exist as though they did** (Romans 4:17).

The revelation that follows, once understood, becomes a powerful advantage for the believer. "*God... gives life to the dead and **calls those things which do not exist as though they did**.*" While God finished with creation on the sixth day, He wasn't done using His words to accomplish His purposes. He chose Abram, made declarations and promises concerning him, and then changed his name to reflect something that hadn't yet happened. Abram was 75 when God promised him a son. He was 99 when God changed his name to mean "a father of many nations," and the promised child had still not been born. God called something which did not exist as though it did. He then proceeded to change the name of Abraham's wife, Sarai.

> *Then God said to Abraham, "As for Sarai your wife, you shall not call her name Sarai, but Sarah shall be her name. And I will bless her and also give you a son by her; then I will bless her, and she shall be a mother of nations"* (Genesis 17:15-16).

An old man and his wife with no children and no biological hope of having children had now received names that did not reflect their current circumstances. They had been called something which did not exist.

What we name things can be a tremendous advantage or a powerful disadvantage. God called for light while there was only darkness. God called for everything visible while it was still invisible to the natural eye. God called Abram a father of many nations while he and his wife were past childbearing years and had no children. What has God called you? Let's look at some examples.

> *No longer do I call you servants, for a servant does not know what his master is doing; but **I have called you friends**, for all things that I heard from My Father I have made known to you* (John 15:15).

To be a friend with God is certainly an advantage in life!

> *To all who are in Rome, beloved of God, **called to be saints*** (Romans 1:7).

This verse literally says that believers are "called saints." The "to be" has been inserted by the translators. We are a new class of men and women, born again and made alive by the Spirit of God!

> *And it shall come to pass in the place where it was said to them, "You are not My people," there **they***

shall be called sons of the living God (Romans 9:26).

While some readers may not "feel" any different, the spiritual reality is true. We have been placed in the family of God, and He is now our Father.

> *But you are a chosen generation, a royal priesthood, a holy nation, His own special people, that you may proclaim the praises of Him who called you out of darkness into His marvelous light* (1 Peter 2:9).

> *Behold what manner of love the Father has bestowed on us, that we should be **called children of God!*** (1 John 3:1)

As friends, saints, sons and daughters, and children of God, the Spirit of God is revealing a new reality that can be enjoyed by the believer. We no longer approach God as distant, mysterious, and temperamental, but as a loving Father. We can now walk and talk with Him as Adam and Eve were meant to do in the Garden of Eden. Religious tradition and rules aren't the goal, but rather a fellowship based on love and trust. Such an understanding removes the insecurity of behavior modification, and moves us into a place of peace and joy. That is an advantage!

You may not feel like a friend of God, a saint, a son or daughter of God, or chosen, royal, holy, and special, but that is what God is calling you. How do you see yourself?

For as he thinks in his heart, so is he (Proverbs 23:7).

If you see yourself and speak of yourself as a fearful victim, unworthy, under resourced, and weak and needy, you are calling things as you see them and enforcing that reality. You are rejecting God's words, which have the power to transform you.

How we name things and call things is important. It can be a matter of life and death. It can be a divine advantage or the continuing of loss and despair.

Are you delivered from the power of darkness, or are you seeking to be delivered?

He has delivered us from the power of darkness *and conveyed us into the kingdom of the Son of His love* (Colossians 1:13).

Are you healed, resisting sickness, or are you sick hoping to get well?

> *Who Himself bore our sins in His own body on the tree, that we, having died to sins, might live for righteousness—**by whose stripes you were healed*** (1 Peter 2:24).

Do you allow yourself to be "named" sick, poor, and helpless? Or will you use the advantage of God's words to declare you are healed, prosperous, and an overcomer?

God is calling things that may not be tangible as though they are. This is so important! If in God's heart we have been delivered and we have been healed, why do we insist that we are in bondage and sick? Would agreeing with God be an advantage? Would calling things as done that we don't see yet with our physical eyes bring change? I know it would. That is how God does things, and we are created in His image.

Are you blessed? Are you loved? Are you filled with joy and peace? Do you have the mind of Christ? How we name, call, and describe things releases power.

> *By faith Moses, when he became of age, **refused to be called** the son of Pharaoh's daughter* (Hebrews 11:24).

Moses refused to be called a son of Pharaoh's daughter, a title that carried esteem, power, and riches. He knew he was truly of Israel, not Egypt.

What we refuse to be called is just as important as what we choose to be called. We often lose our advantages because we take on the names and designations that others give us. When we identify with declarations that are contrary to that which God has declared over us, we are releasing the power of that "name." Even "names" from our childhood could have impacted our development as adults. Negative declarations made over us by parents, teachers, or others could have established conscious or subconscious limitations in our hearts.

Who have you allowed to "name" you and declare your present and future? When it was discovered that I had a softball-sized tumor on my pancreas that was bleeding, cancer in my blood, and that my liver and pancreas had shut down, the doctor advised me to get my affairs in order. As he looked at the scans and other results, he was convinced I had no chance. He called what he saw, and I had to make a decision. Would I receive those words, or would I reject them? The Spirit of God quickened me (a very "still, small voice"), and I had peace that I wouldn't die. That peace and assurance was challenged many times, but saying "no" to death and "yes" to life released the power of God's Word to heal me. That diagnosis was in May of 2020. At this writing I am completely healthy and back to normal life. God's word gave me the advantage in the face of death!

Sometimes "no" is the most powerful word the Spirit will put in your heart. No to fear, no to sickness, no to poverty, no to depression, and no to the influence of the world. Corruption and loss will take as much from your life as you are willing to give. Learn to say "no." Don't call things as you see them and feel them. Call the things that God has promised you as if they are, even if you can't see them or feel them yet. This is your advantage!

Is the challenge in your life a momentary, light affliction, or is it a death sentence?

> *For our light affliction, which is but for a moment, is working for us a far more exceeding and eternal weight of glory* (2 Corinthians 4:17).

Paul named his sufferings for the gospel as a "*light affliction...for a moment.*" How you name things is incredibly important. Whether we are talking about our relationships, our marriage, our children, our job, our finances, or our health, we knowingly or unknowingly are "calling" things and naming them. Declarations such as,

"You'll never amount to anything," "I never have enough money," "My diabetes is killing me," "Nothing ever goes my way," etc. are all destined to fulfill themselves in your life. It's how the Kingdom works. Not only are those who say such things losing their advantage, they are empowering the disadvantage of loss and corruption.

Are you calling things as you see them with your natural eyes, or as you see them through the Word of God? Are you losing your advantage through agreeing with and speaking words of death?

Death and life are in the power of the tongue (Proverbs 18:21).

How we name something, how we define something (incurable cancer, for example), and how we use words to create freedom or bondage will have much to do with our destinies and the quality of our lives.

If you want to enjoy the advantages you have as a child of God, you must learn God's language. Your words are defining and setting the course of your life and future. Are you declaring God's promises over your life, or are you complaining and agreeing with all that is negative? You have the advantage, the gift of God's life-giving words. Believe them and use them!

CHAPTER 6

WHAT DO YOU SEE?

The advantages we have as believers are real and formidable. Why, then, are so many living far below the possibilities that are available? I have found that there are three foundational attitudes that shape the lives of everyone who passes through this earth-life. Our understanding in these three areas can lock us into confusion, bondage, and loss, or can free us into the abundant life that Jesus promised (see John 10:10).

THE GOODNESS OF GOD

How we see God is the most important understanding we can have. Even those who believe there is no God are being shaped by that perception. Those who believe that God is cruel will approach life with that idea. Those who see God as distant, uncaring, or unknowable will have that perception overshadowing how they live. Their perception may not be at the forefront of their minds, but consciously or subconsciously it is there, and it is shaping their lives.

As believers, we have come to know and understand that God is good, God is love, and God became flesh in order to redeem and save us. When we understand the goodness of God, everything about life becomes focused and meaningful. Through my many years of walking with God, I can say that my ever-growing revelation of God's goodness has done more for my faith, joy, and peace than any other revelation. Your faith will always be alive or dormant according to your understanding of His goodness. Let's look at this briefly.

> *I would have lost heart, unless I had believed that I would see **the goodness** of the Lord in the land of the living* (Psalm 27:13).

How our hearts deal with life is directly tied to our perception of God. In this psalm, King David reveals that he was sustained by the knowledge of God's goodness. Though he had no direct knowledge of Jesus and the full revelation of God's goodness that would one day be born into this world, David still understood that seeing God's goodness would determine his future and well-being. How we understand God can be a tremendous advantage or disadvantage in our lives.

How did Jesus reveal the goodness of God? Let's look at some of the things that Jesus said and did to reveal God's goodness.

> *But I say to you, love your enemies, bless those who curse you, do good to those who hate you, and pray for those who spitefully use you and persecute you, that you may be **sons of your Father** in heaven; for **He makes His sun rise on the evil and on the good, and sends rain on the just and on the unjust**** (Matthew 5:44-45).

To be "sons of our Father" implies that we would be like Him. In other words, God loves His enemies, blesses those who curse Him, does good to those who hate Him, and prays for those who persecute Him. This passage is a powerful revelation of God's heart for mankind!

If our perception of God does not include Him being good to the unjust, we lose a huge advantage. It is His goodness that will draw men to Him (Romans 2:4), but if His own children are unsure of this goodness, can they possibly represent Him accurately? He makes His sun and rain available to the evil and unjust!

For He is kind to the unthankful and evil (Luke 6:35).

This can boggle our minds. Why would God be kind to the evil? We often expect God to take up our offenses and judge those who have mistreated us. But that is not God's heart. He desires His children to treat others with goodness.

We are in the age of grace (Hebrews 4:16), the "*acceptable year of the Lord*" (Luke 4:19), and the "today" of salvation (Hebrews 4:7-10). During this "acceptable year," God is for all men. Jesus did not come to destroy men's lives, but to save them.

> *The Lord is not slack concerning His promise, as some count slackness, but is longsuffering toward us, not willing that any should perish but that all should come to repentance* (2 Peter 3:9).

Long-suffering means showing patience in spite of troubles, especially those caused by others. God is not willing that *any* should perish.

Rather than looking for ways to disqualify others from God's love and mercy, we should be loving others as God does with the hope that His love will draw them to Him.

That is our advantage: the love and goodness of God that the world so desperately needs! How did Jesus reveal the true nature of God? Let's begin with Jesus' own words.

He who has seen Me has seen the Father (John 14:9).

*Do you not believe that I am in the Father, and the Father in Me? The words that I speak to you I do not speak on My own authority; but **the Father who dwells in Me does the works*** (John 14:10).

Our perception of God must be centered in Jesus. The Father who dwells in Jesus was responsible for the works that Jesus did.

And when Jesus went out He saw a great multitude; and He was moved with compassion for them, and healed their sick (Matthew 14:14).

God wanted to show His nature and love to a lost and dying humanity. Jesus is the expression of that love and goodness. Compassion is God's goodness in action.

How God anointed Jesus of Nazareth with the Holy Spirit and with power, who went about doing good and healing all who were oppressed by the devil, for God was with Him (Acts 10:38).

Where God is, goodness and healing take place. Few have understood this and many struggle with and even deny this truth. The advantage we have is that we know that we are called to be an expression of His goodness. Jesus made it more than clear.

Most assuredly, I say to you, he who believes in Me, the works that I do he will do also; and greater works than these he will do, because I go to My Father (John 14:12).

We could speak of the goodness of God until Jesus returns. Paul prayed for the believers to have such a revelation.

*That He would grant you, according to the riches of His glory, to be strengthened with might through His Spirit in the inner man, that Christ may dwell in your hearts through faith; that you, being rooted and grounded in love, may be able to comprehend with all the saints what is the width and length and depth and height—**to know the love of Christ which passes knowledge**; that you may* *be filled with all the fullness of God* (Ephesians 3:16-19).

Oh, what an advantage that is available to us! To know the love of Christ which passes knowledge can fill us with the fullness of God. How you see God sets the course of your life.

CHAPTER 7

YOUR PERCEPTION OF YOURSELF

Mankind has been dealing with the impact of Adam's sin throughout history. Fear and uncertainty have shaped the lives of all humans. Because of man's independence from God, all must deal with unhappiness, the lack of peace, stress, and many other emotions that shape our personalities and our approach to life.

Some deal with independence from God by becoming egocentric and self-important, while others become fearful and timid. An image develops on the inside of us all that shapes our personalities and approach to life. *All who remain separated from the life of God are at a disadvantage.*

The true challenge for those who are born again is to grow in the understanding of our new nature and seize the advantage that we have.

Put on the new man who is renewed in knowledge
according to the image of Him who created him
(Colossians 3:10).

This "new man" must be renewed in the knowledge of God who now lives in us. Being a "new creation" "created in righteousness" (see 2 Corinthians 5:17 and Ephesians 4:24) is a life-changing revelation, but if it is not understood or allowed to become our new reality, then the advantage is lost, and life will continue on as if nothing had taken place. We will see ourselves the way we've always seen ourselves and simply take comfort in His forgiveness but leave the rest of the "new man" in a box, undiscovered.

Do you see yourself possessing "*power, love and of a sound mind*" (2 Timothy 1:7)? Have you learned to choose to live by the fruit of the Spirit: love, joy, peace, long-suffering, kindness, goodness, faithfulness, gentleness, and self-control (Galatians 5:22-23)? Do you even believe it is possible to live that way, or have you given up that tremendous advantage only to live by the human emotions and inherent weakness of the "old man"?

When we choose to believe that the Spirit of God is in us, complete with His nature and attributes, we can begin to allow those attributes (the fruit of the Spirit) to shape our lives. We no longer are limited to respond with anger, bitterness, or unforgiveness. We can now choose patience, self-control, love, and joy. This is usually a process of growth over time, but it becomes a huge advantage as we navigate life. The more we exercise the provision of the Spirit, the more it becomes our new default approach to life.

How you see yourself can keep you trapped in the corruption of this world or set you free to live the "abundant life" (John 10:10). The advantages for the believer who comprehends who they are in Christ can't be measured.

The believer who is aware of the presence of God within can have peace and joy in every situation. Fear cannot dominate those who understand their spiritual advantage. The believer is not intimidated by circumstances or people. Just as David showed no signs of fear in the presence of Goliath, the believer can handle the challenges of life with the certainty that God's goodness is more than enough for any situation. You have the advantage!

CHAPTER 8

YOUR PERCEPTION OF CIRCUMSTANCES

Once we understand the advantage of God's goodness and His desire for us to live overcoming lives and we understand the advantage of our new identity in Christ, we can now confront the circumstances of life by the Spirit of God and not through our own strength and limited understanding.

Negative circumstances are an unfortunate reality in a fallen world full of lost and fallen men and women. Not only is the planet suffering under the curse of Adam's sin, but mankind is also suffering under the corruption that was unleashed through that same sin. Sickness, trauma, poverty, despair, depression, destructive weather, economic injustice, war, and fear are all realities that we face frequently. How we respond to these challenges will be based on our vision of God and of ourselves as His children.

The Christian who understands the tremendous advantages of the new birth, the new Kingdom, the power of words, and the heart of God for His children can approach circumstances with a level of faith that the unbelieving and the lost will never understand. While others are resigned to fate, the believer has understood the good, acceptable, and perfect will of God.

> *And do not be conformed to this world, but be transformed by the renewing of your mind, that you may prove what is that good and acceptable and perfect will of God* (Romans 12:2).

As you can see, the life of advantage that I am describing is a proactive life. In spite of the array of challenges that may face us, we are advantaged to see with spiritual eyes and speak spiritual words. Faith is an expression of our fellowship with the Father. Like Jesus, we are called to see what God is doing and act accordingly.

> *I speak to the world those things which I heard from Him* (John 8:26).

> *Then Jesus answered and said to them, "Most assuredly, I say to you, the Son can do nothing of Himself, but what He sees the Father do; for*

whatever He does, the Son also does in like man-
ner" (John 5:19).

This privilege of fellowshipping with the Father and hearing His words and seeing His actions can put us over the top in any circumstance of life. We have been called into fellowship with Him!

God is faithful, by whom you were called into the
fellowship of His Son, Jesus Christ our Lord (1 Corinthians 1:9).

I am not suggesting that we will live free from challenges and problems in this world, but when you understand your advantages as a child of God, your approach to life will be filled with faith and peace rather than fatalism and fear. You have the advantage!

CHAPTER 9

THE ADVANTAGE OF FREEDOM

If there is one word that can describe the advantage of the "new creation" and "Christ in us," it might be the word *freedom*. As I grow in my walk with God, I have discovered freedom on many levels.

There is freedom from the power of sin, freedom from the past, freedom from guilt, freedom from fear, freedom from worry, freedom from lack, freedom from sickness, and freedom from bitterness and offense. Those are pretty good advantages!

But we can go further. There is freedom to love, to give, to forgive, to believe, to trust, to enjoy peace, to have abundant life, and abundant joy!

Freedom is a life-changing revelation. It is meant to be our reality in this life, not just in heaven. The more I meditated on the freedom we have in Him, the more I realized that, yes, God has given us "all things that pertain to life and godliness." We shouldn't accept less than He desires for us.

God is free, and He lives in us. Shouldn't the blessing of freedom be evident in our lives? Shouldn't we be free from strife and offense? Can't we be free to have His joy and peace? Of course, we can. True freedom is found in knowing Him and knowing that He is our life.

> *Therefore if the Son makes you free, you shall be free indeed* (John 8:36).

Obviously, this freedom must be possessed. The world and the enemy will do all it can to steal, kill, and destroy the freedom and joy we have in Christ. We are continually subjected to the voices of the news, of entertainment, of social demands for the acceptance of immorality, of fear over the economy, and many more. You may ask, "How can one be truly free in this fallen world?"

> *Stand fast therefore in the liberty by which Christ has made us free, and do not be entangled again with a yoke of bondage* (Galatians 5:1).

Freedom, peace, and joy are available to you, but you must choose them, and then choose to stand firm in His freedom. Many choose to let the storms of life toss them to and fro, but those who know they have the advantage can choose His peace. We can choose to be free from the stress and pressure of this world. Let it begin in your heart, and it will soon transform your vision, your words, and your faith.

> *You will show me the path of life; in Your presence is fullness of joy* (Psalm 16:11).

Freedom is a powerful advantage in the life of a believer. It should be the stabilizing foundation for a victorious life. When religious bondage, legalism, guilt, and the distractions of life snuff out the freedom that Christ wants us to have, the advantage is lost, and life remains a dull routine.

> *For the law of the Spirit of life in Christ Jesus has made me free from the law of sin and death* (Romans 8:2).

Choose freedom in Christ. See yourself as free to be happy, to have vision, to love unconditionally, to dream, and to give. This advantage will revolutionize your life!

CHAPTER 10

THE BLESSING

As we consider the many ways in which believers have an advantage in life, I want to dig a little deeper and explain that the advantages I'm discussing are all a part of the blessing of God upon His children. While many don't see themselves as blessed, and some might consider their lives as cursed, once we grasp the truth of the blessing, that truth will set us free.

> *Then Jesus said to those Jews who believed Him, "If you abide in My word, you are My disciples indeed. And you shall know the truth, and the truth shall make you free" (John 8:31-32).*

Let's go back to the beginning and see how the blessing began and follow it through time to its ultimate destination—the body of Christ.

*So God created man in His own image; in the image of God He created him; male and female He created them. **Then God blessed them**, and God said to them, "Be fruitful and multiply; fill the earth and subdue it; have dominion over the fish of the sea, over the birds of the air, and over every living thing that moves on the earth"* (Genesis 1:27-28).

We often read over this passage and give little attention to what the blessing of God might mean. God's blessing on Adam and Eve was not simply a "good luck, hope it goes well" kind of thing. It was an empowering and provision to succeed in God's purpose for them: to fill the earth, subdue it, and have dominion.

It is important to remember our previous discussion of the power of words, and how God calls those things that are not as though they were. God's blessing upon Adam and Eve was declared, "*God blessed them, and **God said to them**.*" The power of the blessing was in the words God spoke.

In the Gospels, in each account of Jesus multiplying the loaves and fishes, it mentions that He blessed those elements. The blessing of multiplication was released through His words! Your blessings will be released through your words as well.

The blessing was a spiritual reality that was meant to accompany Adam and Eve everywhere they went and in everything they put their hands to. Everything was going to go their way because it was God's way. God had decreed the blessing.

When Adam and Eve sinned and chose independence from God, not only did they unleash the curse on the earth, but they also lost the blessing. They were on their own. Life would now be a struggle of "good and evil" (the tree they ate from), and the blessing would be limited. Life would be hard.

As we jump forward to the time of Abraham, we see God once again promising a blessing. He spoke to Abraham.

> *Now the Lord had said to Abram: "Get out of your country, from your family and from your father's house, to a land that I will show you. I will make you a great nation; **I will bless you** and make your name great; and you shall be a blessing. I will bless those who bless you, and I will curse him who curses you; and **in you all the families of the earth shall be blessed**"* (Genesis 12:1-3).

For God to accomplish His purpose of redemption and salvation for mankind, He had to begin with a man, and He had to speak to that man and about that man. God's purposes are accomplished by words. God had given the earth to man, and man's redemption would have to be accomplished through a man. Abraham was chosen to be the man through whom God would eventually bring forth the "Seed" who would bless the nations: Jesus, the Son of Man, Son of God.

God's heart was to restore the blessing to mankind. He began with Abraham. I won't take the time to develop the full story of Abram/Abraham, but let us consider the effects of the blessing that God pronounced upon him.

> *Abram was very rich in livestock, in silver, and in gold* (Genesis 13:2).

> *For all the land which you see I give to you and your descendants forever* (Genesis 13:15).

> *After these things the word of the Lord came to Abram in a vision, saying, "Do not be afraid, Abram. I am your shield, your exceedingly great reward"* (Genesis 15:1).

*And he believed in the Lord, and He accounted it
to him for righteousness* (Genesis 15:6).

In just these four verses, we can glean a tremendous
revelation of what the blessing of God means. The
blessing of God on Abraham made him rich, gave him
an inheritance forever, protected him, rewarded him, and
established him in righteousness by faith! Abraham had
an advantage!

How does that impact us today?

*Know ye therefore that they which are of faith, the
same are the children of Abraham* (Galatians 3:7
KJV).

Did you know that the blessing that was upon Abraham
is now upon all who have faith in the finished work of the
cross?

*So then those who are of faith are blessed with
believing Abraham* (Galatians 3:9).

Most of us have very little understanding of what this
means. We may evaluate our lives and conclude that there
is little evidence of the blessing. What are we missing? To
begin with, the blessing is by faith.

Many Christians have believed for forgiveness but have never entered into all that is available by faith. It would be like receiving a free ticket to an amusement park for the day and then just sitting at the entrance. You would have access to all the rides and entertainment, but you wouldn't enjoy any of it because you didn't understand that when you received the ticket, you received the blessing of the entire amusement park. Many Christians live at the front door of the blessing but never enter in. Some are even taught that it would be wrong to expect such a blessing. Again, our perception of God so often limits our experience in life.

Let's unwrap more of this blessing.

> *Christ has redeemed us from the curse of the law, having become a curse for us (for it is written, "Cursed is everyone who hangs on a tree"), that the blessing of Abraham might come upon the Gentiles in Christ Jesus, that we might receive the promise of the Spirit through faith* (Galatians 3:13-14).

Wow! Not only have we entered into a blessing, we have been redeemed from a curse! What does this mean? The "curse of the law" refers specifically to the consequences that Israel would suffer for their lack of obedience to God and His Word (the Law of Moses). Sadly, many today still live with the mindset of blessings and curses based on their behavior, and most realize that they can't measure up, so they feel they deserve the curses and hardships of life.

But praise God, our better covenant with God is a result of Jesus' behavior, not ours! Jesus lived a sinless life; defeated temptation, sin, and the devil; and as an exclamation point, He defeated death. And His victory is our advantage, our blessing! When we believed in this redemptive work of Christ, we entered into the "blessing of Abraham" that God had promised thousands of years ago. By faith the Spirit of God has quickened our spirit and made the blessing available. The blessing is ours!

The curse that includes everything that Adam's sin unleashed has been nailed to the cross. Everything that was against you, including all of your failures, sins, and fears, has been removed and done away with. You have the advantage! You have the blessing!

Having wiped out the handwriting of requirements that was against us, which was contrary to us. And He has taken it out of the way, having nailed it to the cross (Colossians 2:14).

If there is nothing against you, you are blessed. You have the advantage! While unbelievers struggle with guilt and fear, you are free to enjoy peace with God. You are free to walk in His joy!

Paul spoke of the reality of this blessing.

> *Blessed be the God and Father of our Lord Jesus Christ, who has blessed us with every spiritual blessing in the heavenly places in Christ* (Ephesians 1:3).

Paul understood that this Gospel message, the Good News, was not just an escape from hell but also an empowerment for the abundant life of which Jesus spoke.

> *The thief does not come except to steal, and to kill, and to destroy. I have come that they may have life, and that they may have it more abundantly* (John 10:10).

Paul understood the abundant life to be the blessing of God.

> *But I know that when I come to you, I shall come in **the fullness of the blessing of the gospel of Christ*** (Romans 15:29).

Peter understood the blessing when he wrote:

*Not returning evil for evil or reviling for reviling, but on the contrary blessing, knowing that you were called to this, **that you may inherit a blessing** (1 Peter 3:9).*

What does this blessing mean for us? What does this inheritance look like?

__Blessed__ are those whose lawless deeds are forgiven, and whose sins are covered; __blessed__ is the man to whom the Lord shall not impute sin (Romans 4:7-8).

If you have been forgiven and sin is not being imputed unto you, you are blessed. You are free from guilt, condemnation, and fear.

For God has not given us a spirit of fear, but of power and of love and of a sound mind (2 Timothy 1:7).

What an advantage! Whether you know it or not, your born-again spirit has no fear but is a spirit of power, love, and a sound mind. Are you living in the blessing? Have you believed the advantage?

The sooner we accept and believe that we are blessed, the more quickly we will be able to be a blessing to others.

The more we walk in the joy of the Lord, the more we can spread His joy to others. The more we live in freedom from guilt, the more we can minister that freedom to others. The blessing transforms you from victim to victor. The blessing opens your spiritual eyes to see the possibilities and not just the problems.

While others think they need to be delivered, you know that you have been delivered!

> *He has delivered us from the power of darkness and conveyed us into the kingdom of the Son of His love* (Colossians 1:13).

The blessing is upon you in everything you do if you will believe it. Only our unbelief and self-condemnation keeps us from enjoying the power of His blessing.

All of the promises of God for His children past and present are "yes and amen."

> *For all the promises of God in Him are Yes, and in Him Amen, to the glory of God through us* (2 Corinthians 1:20).

When you understand the blessing, you begin to read the Bible with new eyes. You are no longer reading from the Tree of the Knowledge of Good and Evil, but from the Tree of Life. You see His goodness all throughout the Word. You see blessings, promises, and potential. You have the advantage!

CHAPTER 11

FAVOR WITH GOD!

We often look at the lives of the rich and powerful and wonder what it would be like to live as they seem to live. What would it be like to have others working for you, taking care of every need? Many daydream of such things but don't believe that they are smart enough or gifted enough to ever have such a life. However, as children of God, we have promises that transcend the temporal world. We have the favor of God on our lives. We have the advantage!

For You, O Lord, will bless the righteous; with favor You will surround him as with a shield (Psalm 5:12).

What a promise! Can it be true? Do we expect the kindness and provision of God to be around us like a shield? Again, our perception of God and our perception of ourselves will set the boundaries of how much of this advantage we experience.

It seems the first condition is to be righteous. "*For You, O Lord, will bless the righteous.*" Do you qualify for blessing and favor? Are you righteous? Let's look at what the apostle Paul had to say about righteousness.

> *For if by the one man's offense death reigned through the one, much more those who receive abundance of grace and of **the gift of righteousness** will reign in life through the One, Jesus Christ* (Romans 5:17).

This incredible declaration from Paul not only establishes the promise of favor found in Psalm 5 but adds the idea of "reigning in life" through Jesus. The "gift of righteousness" is the key. Righteousness (right standing with God, free from sin, a new creation) is a gift. You can't earn it, but if you have by faith received this gift, you can reign in life. You are surrounded with favor as with a shield!

Perhaps the most powerful revelation in my life as a young Christian was the revelation of the gift of righteousness. That revelation was a key to setting me free from guilt, fear, and unworthiness. Those feelings are a tremendous disadvantage for victorious living, but when one understands righteousness, the possibilities are endless. The advantage becomes real.

None of us can clean up our lives enough to be righteous in the eyes of God. God in His love knew we were helpless. That is why Jesus came to redeem us. We were like a lost and starving dog that someone saved and made their own. The dog can't repay the gift of life, but it can certainly enjoy the benefits! That is what makes a gift a gift. How did Isaiah see this blessing?

> *"No weapon formed against you shall prosper, and every tongue which rises against you in judgment you shall condemn. This is the heritage of the servants of the Lord,* **and their righteousness is from Me,***" says the Lord* (Isaiah 54:17).

Isaiah could have said, "This is the advantage of the servants of the Lord," or, "This is the advantage of those who have received My gift." We have inherited God's favor. It is like a shield that surrounds us. We should expect good things. A positive expectation in life should be our daily reality. And our righteousness is not based on how good we are, but rather on how good Jesus is. By faith we enter into His blessing, favor, and His advantage.

A few years ago, I was driving to work (Charis Bible College), and it was early and dark. As I merged onto the highway and reached 75 miles per hour, I noticed the taillights of a car ahead of me jerk to one side. The next thing I knew, I saw a deer immediately in front of my car, and with no time to swerve, I hit the deer. As I was trying to maintain control and slow down, I said out loud to no one, "This shouldn't be happening to me!" In that moment I found that my "default" approach to life was one of a positive expectation. I don't expect bad things to happen. That doesn't mean they never will, but it's not my expectation. I expect good things. I didn't lose my cool and "freak out." I know that God is my Source.

I was not hurt in the accident, but my car was totaled. But I have favor with God! With the insurance settlement, some other blessings, and a good deal from the dealer, within a week I was driving a brand-new car! Favor surrounds me. I believe it and I declare it all of the time.

I know some may scoff at such an attitude, but I make no apologies. I have believed in the gift of righteousness, and I expect God's favor. The accident with the deer did not prosper against me. A few years later, a doctor's declaration that I was near death and should get my affairs in order did not prosper against me. I was shocked and confused, but not despairing. God is my Source and I expect favor. Other situations in life that could have been serious have not prospered against me. I have the advantage. You have the advantage if you will believe you have God's favor.

Favor is the blessing of God that opens doors, gives protection, promotes, and provides for those who will believe it. How can we walk in favor with God and man? As we have seen, understanding and receiving the gift of righteousness is the first step.

> *For You, O Lord, will bless the righteous; with favor You will surround him as with a shield* (Psalm 5:12).

Let's look at some other characteristics that empower us to walk in God's favor.

> *He who earnestly seeks good finds favor* (Proverbs 11:27).

Living to be a blessing, to give, to forgive, and to do good is a key to finding favor both from God and from others.

> *Let not mercy and truth forsake you; bind them around your neck, write them on the tablet of your*

heart, and so find favor and high esteem in the sight of God and man (Proverbs 3:3-4).

Being merciful and addicted to the *truth* will release favor in your life.

Again, I am not saying that there will never be challenges and there will never be persecution. But even in the midst of such circumstances, we can know that God is for us, and we can expect the best while others might be discouraged and depressed.

Good understanding gains favor, but the way of the unfaithful is hard (Proverbs 13:15).

Having a good understanding of the ways of God brings favor. It is a lack of knowledge that makes life hard for so many believers. They don't have a good understanding of God and His promises. If we add unfaithfulness into the mix, life gets hard.

Peter gives us a tremendous revelation as to how the favor of God can be released in our lives.

Grace and peace be multiplied to you in the knowledge of God and of Jesus our Lord, as His divine power has given to us all things that pertain to life and godliness, through the knowledge of Him who called us by glory and virtue, by which have been given to us exceedingly great and precious promises, that through these you may be partakers of the divine nature, having escaped the corruption that is in the world through lust (2 Peter 1:2-4).

The word *grace* is the Greek word *charis*. It is a word of several meanings and includes all of God's provision for His children, from spiritual gifts to goodwill, loving-kindness, strength, and favor. How is this grace and favor multiplied in our lives? Through the knowledge of God and Jesus.

How we see God, either as a loving Father or a demanding dictator, will determine what we expect in life and whether or not it we must live in our own limited strength or in the favor of God.

God's divine power has given us all things (grace) that pertain to life and godliness, through the knowledge of Him. How is this grace and favor released in our lives? *Through His exceedingly great and precious promises.* The purpose of God's favor (His promises) is that we escape the corruption that is in the world through lust. He has given us the advantage!

We can see the darkness and corruption of the world every day. We have all experienced challenges and loss to some degree. Those circumstances are not God's will for us. It is the enemy who comes to steal, kill, and destroy (John 10:10). Jesus came to give us abundant life. To escape corruption and experience abundant life, we need His favor. His favor is alive in His promises!

As you read God's words in the scriptures, pay attention to the promises and declarations He has made concerning His children—those who love Him. Regardless of when the promise was made or the context, there is a concept of God's goodness and His intentions that are revealed in every promise. All of His promises are "yes and amen"!

> *For all the promises of God in Him are Yes, and in Him Amen, to the glory of God through us* (2 Corinthians 1:20).

When we understand God's heart and His goodness, we will begin to see His promises as relevant to us. His promises of health, provision, increase, influence, forgiveness, safety, and blessing are all "yes and amen"! That is His favor, and that is our advantage!

DECLARATION

God is blessing me today. All grace is abounding in my life. I have favor in all that I do. I have peace with God and His joy is my strength. I am filled with His love and there is no fear in my heart.

CHAPTER 12

YOU CAN HEAR GOD!

We have been created to hear God. We were created in His image with the capacity to hear His voice. Even after Adam sinned, he was still able to hear the voice of God as He walked in the Garden (Genesis 3:8-10). Though communion was lost and mankind entered into darkness, the capacity to hear God was not lost. God is seeking to communicate with every person on earth.

> *I will hear what God the Lord will speak* (Psalm 85:8).

On the battlefield, the disruption of communication between the generals and the soldiers can be disastrous. Soldiers who don't know the goals, strategies, and tactics of their leaders can be easily defeated.

It is the same in the battle of life. The advantage for the believer is the potential to hear God on a daily and even moment-by-moment basis. Our fellowship with the Father is vital to our success in life. All the money in the world is not worth the advantage of fellowshipping with God and hearing Him. This gift is beyond human understanding.

The sad thing is that many Christians don't take advantage of the advantage, and then wonder why they are always losing or suffering in their challenges.

Just because God lives in you does not mean you are hearing Him or in fellowship with Him. Proximity does not create fellowship. Many married couples can understand this. Living in the same house or being in the same car does not mean a couple is enjoying fellowship. Though God lives in every believer, there may be no true fellowship. Fellowship must be intentional.

It is God's grace that gives every man the opportunity to hear Him. It is man's great loss that he often seeks meaning and purpose in life through things created rather than in the Creator.

> *Because, although they knew God, they did not glorify Him as God, nor were thankful, but became futile in their thoughts, and their foolish hearts were darkened* (Romans 1:21).

Jesus mentioned this same problem with the Jews to whom He had come to reveal God.

> *For the hearts of this people have grown dull. Their ears are hard of hearing, and their eyes they have closed, lest they should see with their eyes and hear with their ears, lest they should understand with their hearts and turn, so that I should heal them* (Matthew 13:15).

Notice that they had closed their eyes and they had allowed their ears to become dull. It isn't that God has stopped speaking; it is that most of us are so preoccupied with the issues of life that we have given little time or attention to hearing Him. And yet, we were created to hear Him and to live by every word that proceeds from His mouth. That is the advantage!

> *But He answered and said, "It is written, 'Man shall not live by bread alone, but by every word that proceeds from the mouth of God'"* (Matthew 4:4).

Hearing God should be as normal as eating! All men are spiritual beings created in the image of God and all men have the capacity to hear Him. Our re-born spirits are created to *live* in contact with God.

*For what man knows the things of a man except the spirit of the man which is in him? Even so no one knows the things of God except the Spirit of God. **Now we have received**, not the spirit of the world, but **the Spirit who is from God**, that we might know the things that have been freely given to us by God* (1 Corinthians 2:11-12).

What an incredible advantage! God wants to communicate with you! He wants to show you all that has become yours through Christ. He wants to bring you out of despair, discouragement, fear, sickness, and poverty into the abundant life. This goes beyond the general revelation of Himself that is available to all through creation. This is the specific revelation to our re-created spirits that we might know the greatness of our inheritance in Him. God wants to teach you, give you wisdom, prepare you, warn you, and deliver you. He is speaking! Why aren't many hearing Him?

But the natural man does not receive the things of the Spirit of God, for they are foolishness to him; nor can he know them, because they are spiritually discerned (1 Corinthians 2:14).

Sadly, many Christians could be classified as natural men, not because they aren't born again, but because they simply give no time to the things of God. The cares of this world have choked the Word and they have chosen to live as natural men, not spiritual.

Consider the challenge of the blind and the deaf. In the natural world they are certainly at a disadvantage. The sights and sounds that most take for granted are unknown to those who cannot see or hear. It is a different life that they live. Adjustments are made, but the rich world of sight and sound remains locked away and only imagined.

The "natural man" is living a similar life. A life without hearing God is a minimal existence at best. We were created to hear Him. Choosing to ignore Him and live life on the natural level is like being blind and deaf at the same time. You can adjust, but you will never know the abundant life. The advantage is lost.

Sadly, there are many natural Christians who aren't really hearing God or having His truths revealed to their spirits. Paul explained how this hearing takes place.

> *The Spirit Himself bears witness with our spirit* (Romans 8:16).

The things of the Kingdom are contained in scripture, but they are only revealed from Spirit to spirit—from His to ours. The disciples (and all believers) are privileged to receive the revelation of the things of God.

> *And He said to them, "To you it has been given to know the mystery of the kingdom of God; but to those who are outside, all things come in parables"* (Mark 4:11).

Paul said:

> *But we speak the wisdom of God in a mystery, the hidden wisdom which God ordained before the ages for our glory* (1 Corinthians 2:7).

In other words, there are things God wants us to know and mysteries He wants to reveal. This is not impossible or even difficult. It is His will. But if we haven't created the environment to hear Him, we will have to live without.

> *However, when He, the Spirit of truth, has come, He will guide you into all truth; for He will not speak on His own authority, but whatever He hears He will speak; and He will tell you things to come* (John 16:13).

As long as we have no interest in hearing from God, vanity and ignorance will be our environment *even if we are born again!* Just because the Spirit of God lives within does not mean that the mysteries of God and His promises will automatically be real to us. This advantage must be valued and accessed.

What transpired when you became a "new creation"?

> *Therefore, if anyone is in Christ, he is a new creation; old things have passed away; behold, all things have become new* (2 Corinthians 5:17).

> *For you were once darkness, but now you are light in the Lord. Walk as children of light* (Ephesians 5:8).

That which Adam lost for all mankind has been restored through Christ. We not only walked in darkness, we *were* darkness. Spiritual revelation was not possible as it is now. But in Christ we have been plugged back into the Source and we are light. In other words, the light of life has entered and transformed our spirits. We are once again in a position to have communion with God. We can hear Him with our spirits!

God wants to reveal things to us, from the smallest details of life to the greatest revelations of Kingdom mysteries. It is all available to our spirits. The question is, have we made ourselves available to be quickened by His Spirit? Do we really want the advantage?

CHAPTER 13

FELLOWSHIP WITH GOD

L et's go a little deeper into this tremendous blessing of hearing God.

In the beginning it was God's intention to walk and talk with Adam and Eve, and no doubt with all who would be born thereafter. Fellowship with God was to be the purpose and priority of His creation and the means by which God would influence man's reign over the planet.

As born-again believers, we have the tremendous privilege and advantage of renewing that potential and receiving direction, wisdom, and purpose directly from Him. Fellowship with God is once again possible.

> *And truly our fellowship is with the Father and with His Son Jesus Christ* (1 John 1:3).

God is faithful, by whom you were called into the fellowship of His Son, Jesus Christ our Lord (1 Corinthians 1:9).

I want to use the word *fellowship* instead of the word *prayer* because the traditional thinking about prayer can restrict and even hinder the advantage that we have. Walking and talking with God in Eden was actually what has now been shaped into religious duty and even a mystery that many dread.

While prayer is spoken of at length in the Bible, the potential has often been lost in the baggage of religion. Jesus spent great amounts of time fellowshipping with the Father, and in fact, His ministry, miracles, and teachings all came from that fellowship.

Then Jesus answered and said to them, "Most assuredly, I say to you, the Son can do nothing of Himself, but what He sees the Father do; for whatever He does, the Son also does in like manner" (John 5:19).

Have you understood prayer to include "seeing" what the Father is doing? What if your fellowship with Him included *seeing* the eternal heart of God for you and those around you?

While we do not look at the things which are seen, but at the things which are not seen. For the things which are seen are temporary, but the things which are not seen are eternal (2 Corinthians 4:18).

Wouldn't it be an incredible advantage to see the works of God while fellowshipping with Him. Is that possible? Absolutely, but it is a fellowship that must be nurtured and valued to produce such fruit. Jesus said it this way:

For the Father loves the Son, and shows Him all things that He Himself does; and He will show Him greater works than these, that you may marvel (John 5:20).

This is *true prayer*. From Jesus' words above, it seems to be a result of God's love for Jesus and His willingness to show and do great works through Him. Does the Father love you? Let's see how Jesus prayed for us shortly before His arrest.

*I in them, and You in Me; that they may be made perfect in one, and that the world may know that **You have sent Me, and have loved them as You have loved Me*** (John 17:23).

The Father loves you as much as He loves Jesus! Would He also show you His will and His works? Has He sent you?

So Jesus said to them again, "Peace to you! As the Father has sent Me, I also send you" (John 20:21).

If He loves us as He loves Jesus and has sent us as He sent Jesus, then shouldn't it be possible that in our fellowship with Him, He would also show us His will and His works? Wouldn't that be an advantage?

No longer do I call you servants, for a servant does not know what his master is doing; but I have called you friends, for all things that I heard from My Father I have made known to you (John 15:15).

Many times in my walk with God I have been shown things to come, been encouraged in the present circumstances, and even been warned of potential danger. As I look back, I can now see more clearly that it was my heart for God and my fellowship with Him that allowed my spirit to be quickened with His divine communication. Fellowship with God is the source of true faith.

So then faith comes by hearing, and hearing by the word of God (Romans 10:17).

Fellowship with God has saved my life, prospered me, and made me a vessel for blessing others. When you are sensitive to God, you will be more sensitive to the needs around you, and because you have "seen" His works, you can release faith into those circumstances. This is what true prayer is all about.

Fellowship with the Father is the door into the abundant life. Hearing Him is the most valuable potential that we have. It is the key to being a blessing in this earth. Those who choose to value this fellowship will find themselves living life in a different dimension. No longer are we helpless victims, mired in the uncertainty of life, begging God for crumbs from His table. We are now *friends* with God, included in His "inner circle," receiving vision, revelation, wisdom, and direction while in fellowship with Him!

This is seldom what is taught today, but it is what is taught in God's Word. You and I have been called into fellowship with God, and that fellowship is the source of the abundant life.

I am the vine, you are the branches. He who abides in Me, and I in him, bears much fruit; for without Me you can do nothing (John 15:5).

Don't be without Him! Don't waste the advantage. The Father wants to walk and talk with you.

CHAPTER 14

THE ADVANTAGE OF PEACE WITH GOD

I have come to realize that many Christians are more fearful of God than truly enjoy Him. So often believers are questioning their salvation, aware of the struggles in their hearts, and unsure if God accepts them or not. Is that the relationship Jesus died for—uncertainty, guilt, and stress? I don't believe so.

> *Do not fear, little flock, for it is your Father's good pleasure to give you the kingdom* (Luke 12:32).

Fear is a powerful disadvantage. When we live in fear, whether it is an unhealthy fear of God, a fear of circumstances, or a fear of our own flesh, we undermine the advantage of the abundant life and our fellowship with the Father. We must leave the baggage of religious thinking behind and begin to see God as He really is. It gives God pleasure to give you His Kingdom! Jesus came that we might have life more abundantly. Shouldn't that be a positive experience?

> *For the kingdom of God is not eating and drinking, but righteousness and peace and joy in the Holy Spirit* (Romans 14:17).

Freedom from guilt accompanied by peace and joy in the Spirit sounds like a good deal! Is that your experience and approach to your fellowship with Him? The Kingdom of God is *peace*. We have discussed righteousness, but let's talk about peace.

A few years ago, I was studying the subject of heaven. I had looked up all the verses I could find about what happens to a believer after they depart this life on earth. I had been meditating on the subject for a couple of weeks when one night I turned on an old TV show from the '80s in which the star died but didn't know he had died. He suddenly found himself on a beautiful beach enjoying himself without a care in the world. In that brief moment, the Lord revealed to me what awaits believers when they transition to the presence of the Lord. I saw absolute peace. No cares, no fear, and every need and want provided for in abundance.

It was a two or three second "revelation" that captured my heart. I turned off the TV and began to think about what I had "seen" in my spirit. As I considered the power of that revelation, I said to the Lord, "I want that." In my spirit the Lord responded, "Barry, you can have that now." As I meditated longer, I realized it was true! I don't have to live in fear, worry, and anxiety. I can experience righteousness, peace, and joy now. Jesus declared it!

Peace I leave with you, My peace I give to you; not as the world gives do I give to you. Let not your heart be troubled, neither let it be afraid (John 14:27).

Though we live in a world full of darkness and corruption, there is light and life for those who want it. God is a giving God. In place of our weakness and lack, God gives strength. In the midst of the turmoil around us, God gives us peace.

The Lord will give strength to His people; the Lord will bless His people with peace (Psalm 29:11).

His peace is not dependent on outward circumstances. His peace can sustain you regardless of what is going on around you. You can have His peace in the midst of any circumstances. It is the quiet confidence that God is on your side and will deliver you.

Jesus was at peace, asleep in the boat in the midst of a storm that was fierce enough to cause the disciples to believe they were going to die! And yet, Jesus slept.

> *And a great windstorm arose, and the waves beat into the boat, so that it was already filling. But He was in the stern, asleep on a pillow. And they awoke Him and said to Him, "Teacher, do You not care that we are perishing?"*
>
> *Then He arose and rebuked the wind, and said to the sea, "Peace, be still!" And the wind ceased and there was a great calm* (Mark 4:37-39).

Isn't it interesting that Jesus' words to the storm began with the word *peace*? From a place of peace, Jesus used the advantage of peace, spoke peace, and there was peace. And He has given us His peace!

This is a tremendous advantage in life. While others are anxious, fearful, depressed, and worried about the country, the economy, the culture, and all of the darkness around us, we have His peace. What an advantage! In fact, His peace is a powerful weapon against the works of the enemy!

And the God of peace will crush Satan under your feet shortly. The grace of our Lord Jesus Christ be with you. Amen (Romans 16:20).

Notice that Paul refers to God as the "God of peace," and then continues by using a word of violence to describe Satan's end! God's peace crushes the works of darkness that want to steal, kill, and destroy your life. His peace is a powerful advantage. The lost don't know His peace, but you can.

Peace is actually a part of His nature within us. Consider the fruit of the Spirit that believers receive when they are born again.

*But the fruit of the Spirit is love, joy, **peace**, longsuffering, kindness, goodness, faithfulness, gentleness, self-control* (Galatians 5:22-23).

Are you taking advantage of this advantage? Are you choosing His peace in the circumstances of your life. It is a spiritual power that can overwhelm the chaos of life. How can we know and live in His peace?

You will keep him in perfect peace, whose mind is stayed on You, because he trusts in You (Isaiah 26:3).

An uncontrolled mind that allows the never-ending flood of news and carnal entertainment to occupy the thought life will not know peace. The advantage and the power of that advantage will be lost. Paul gives us a tremendous exhortation concerning how to stay in His peace.

> *Be anxious for nothing, but in everything by prayer and supplication, with thanksgiving, let your requests be made known to God; and **the peace of God, which surpasses all understanding,** will guard your hearts and minds through Christ Jesus* (Philippians 4:6-7).

Our prayer and fellowship with the Father should consume far more of our time than the darkness of this world. How we spend our time and what or who we "fellowship" with will determine the level of our peace. For many, the advantage of His peace is often lost. Paul goes on in this same chapter of Philippians:

> *Finally, brethren, whatever things are true, whatever things are noble, whatever things are just, whatever things are pure, whatever things are lovely, whatever things are of good report, if there is any virtue and if there is anything praiseworthy—meditate on these things* (Philippians 4:8).

A mind that is dedicated to things that are pure, true, and noble will be a mind filled with God's peace. Bad news won't overwhelm the peace of God. In fact, the peace of God is the foundation for overcoming bad news. The peace the world gives is circumstantial and very temporary. It comes and goes based on immediate events in one's life but is very fragile and fleeting. The peace of God is a foundation for living that will not be shaken. It is your powerful advantage!

Peace is strength.

The Lord will give strength to His people; the Lord will bless His people with peace (Psalm 29:11).

Peace is safety.

I will both lie down in peace, and sleep; for You alone, O Lord, make me dwell in safety (Psalm 4:8).

His peace is your powerful advantage!

CHAPTER 15

THE ADVANTAGE OF AN IMAGE

A dvertisers are well aware of the power of images. They carefully create pictures of their products for TV, magazines, billboards, etc. The idea is that the picture will create an image within the viewer that will in turn create a desire and hopefully a decision to pursue or buy what is being advertised. Images can be very effective.

Images in the news can create sadness, anger, the desire to get involved, or the desire to stay away from whatever is being seen.

In Jesus' day, there was no advertising as we know it; however, Jesus used images to teach His followers. He spoke of the lilies of the field, the farmer sowing seed, wine and wineskins, leaven and bread, sheep and shepherds, and more. Jesus knew that creating an image could change a heart.

When we think of a "vision" from the Lord, we often think of an open vision that plays before us like a movie, but those seldom happen for most believers. What happens in your thought life on a daily basis is the vision or image you carry in your heart.

> *For as he thinks in his heart, so is he* (Proverbs 23:7).

We each have images within that shape our lives. As I have discussed earlier in this book, we have an image of God, we have an image of ourselves, and we have an image of our circumstances. The picture on the inside shapes the thoughts, words, and actions of our lives. How accurate are the images that we carry within? Are the images in your heart an advantage or a disadvantage?

Ministry is the grace of God to change the images within you to match the images that God has for you. The vision of your heart sets the course of your life. Consider Jesus' words in Matthew 12.

> *A good man out of the good treasure of his heart brings forth good things, and an evil man out of the evil treasure brings forth evil things* (Matthew 12:35).

Instantly we can see that this "treasure" can be a good thing or a bad thing. It is from this treasure that we either have an advantage or disadvantage.

The "treasure" is the image or vision you carry within. It can be a treasure of faith, hope, love, and victory, or it can be a treasure of doubt, fear, and loss. You have an image inside of you, whether you have given it much thought or not. From that image or "treasure" you are living your life.

A negative doctor's report can create a vision of impending death, but the word of God can overwhelm that vision with an image of healing and health. Which image will win? Only you can decide what you will see in your heart.

The disciples had an image of lack when faced with feeding the multitudes. They made sure that Jesus understood how bad the situation was. *"And they said to Him, 'We have here only five loaves and two fish'"* (Matthew 14:17). Jesus carried a different image on the inside. He thanked the Father for what He had, blessed it, and put it to work. Thousands were fed because Jesus had a different image of the possibilities. His vision was His advantage.

Do you see yourself as God sees you? Do you see yourself full of faith, full of joy, and full of love? Do you see a powerful man or woman of God inside of you, or do you still see a fearful, insecure victim?

So much of our life is spent evaluating. We evaluate our health, we evaluate our economic condition, we evaluate our marriage, our children, our job, and our country. The list could go on.

Most evaluation focuses on what we see, hear, and feel about situations and people. We are very locked into that which is tangible. Those evaluations create images on the inside. Those images shape our attitudes, thoughts, and words. Attitudes, thoughts, and words are the seeds of our future.

Our image/treasure is subject to how much of God's Word finds a place in our hearts. What you meditate on is what you will "see." What you see in your heart will become your destiny.

> *For I know the thoughts that I think toward you, says the Lord, thoughts of peace and not of evil, to give you a future and a hope* (Jeremiah 29:11).

God has a vision for your life. The thoughts of the treasure of God's heart are not evil. Jesus made it clear when He declared that He came to give us life in abundance (see John 10:10). Many see their walk with God as uncertain and filled with preordained tests and trials. The advantage of God's desire for a victorious life is lost.

The more that your images come from God and accurately reflect His nature, your life in Him, and His grace for your circumstances, the more you will experience His abundant life.

Probably the most powerful image you carry within is your image of God. That image will determine almost everything else in your life. It can be an advantage that gives you continual victory or a disadvantage that keeps you in bondage. If you see God as controlling, you will succumb to fatalism. If you see God as judging every mistake, you will always feel unworthy. If you don't believe there is a God, you will become your own god. What image should a believer have of God in his heart?

If you had known Me, you would have known My Father also; and from now on you know Him and have seen Him (John 14:7).

He who has seen Me has seen the Father (John 14:9).

God knows the importance of images. If we are going to truly know and appreciate God for who He is, we need to leave the fog of religion and look on His image.

His Son...who being the brightness of His glory and the express image of His person (Hebrews 1:2-3).

If you have seen Jesus, you have seen the Father. Jesus is the express image of God. God wanted us to see Himself, so He became flesh and lived among us (see John 1:14).

Some say that God is mysterious and no one can know Him. But the mystery is resolved! Jesus is God in the flesh. Jesus is the express image of God. Why is this important? Because now, we no longer have an excuse to misunderstand God and blame Him for our woes. Jesus only did what He saw the Father doing, and only spoke what He heard the Father speaking. He came to do God's will and reveal God to humanity.

How God anointed Jesus of Nazareth with the Holy Spirit and with power, who went about doing good and healing all who were oppressed by the devil, for God was with Him (Acts 10:38).

God does good and heals all. Is that your image of Him? The image of God in your heart will set the course for your life. Either He is loving, merciful, and good, or He is angry, judgmental, and controlling. What do you see?

It is the Truth that will set us free. Ministry is replacing the lying images of your past with the images of Truth that can propel you into a life of righteousness, peace, and joy in the Holy Spirit. Be open to a new picture. One picture can change your life.

CHAPTER 16

THE ADVANTAGE OF JOY

I have seen many times the reaction of children when they find themselves in a large, unfurnished ballroom or an immense park with nothing but grass. They immediately begin squealing with delight and running and running. What is prompting this joy? They feel free! There are no limitations, no obstructions, and no barriers to their ability to run and play. There is something about freedom that fills the heart with joy.

We know that the fruit of the Spirit includes joy (Galatians 5:22), and when we understand, *"Now the Lord is the Spirit; and where the Spirit of the Lord is, there is liberty"* (2 Corinthians 3:17), we begin to see the potential for joy! The same Spirit that gives us liberty to walk and talk with God, be free from guilt, hear Him speak, see His blessings, and speak His words fills us with His joy.

Can you see yourself as a child running and laughing to your heart's content? That advantage is real for those who believe it and receive it. His joy is a powerful resource in a world filled with misery.

Rejoice in the Lord always (Philippians 4:4).

Do you enjoy your walk with God, or are you always unsure of where you stand with Him? Are you more conscious of your failings or of His love and grace?

Delight yourself also in the Lord (Psalm 37:4).

Those who are sin conscious are always evaluating their behavior and the behavior of others. Those who are God conscious are free to delight themselves in His goodness. You can tell who is free and who is bound up in guilt and fear. You can see it on the faces and hear it in the words. The advantage of freedom and joy is palpable.

You will show me the path of life; in Your presence is fullness of joy; at Your right hand are pleasures forevermore (Psalm 16:11).

Too often our church traditions have snuffed out freedom and joy. Sadly, many religious doctrines do more to constrict the life of a believer than to set them free. As a result, joy is lost. There is no joy in feeling guilty and unworthy. There is no joy in feeling obligated to perform religious duties. I'm not suggesting that our freedom includes a freedom to chase after the flesh, but I am saying that our walk with God should be one of joy, and if it isn't, there is some freedom missing somewhere.

To the degree that you have peace with God and enjoy Him, you will be an expression of His love to others. When you know He loves you, you share what you have received. Joyful believers are contagious. Choose to enjoy the gift of salvation, the gift of righteousness, the blessing of hearing Him, and start living!

> *Do not sorrow, for the joy of the Lord is your strength* (Nehemiah 8:10).

The advantage of joy is strength. Not our own strength, but the supernatural strength that flows from the Spirit who gives liberty, love, joy, peace, and all the rest. What an advantage to be free to enjoy the goodness of God and share His goodness with joy! Don't let religious traditions and structures steal your joy. No joy, no strength. We have the advantage, but we must persevere to maintain it.

> *Let them shout for joy and be glad, who favor my righteous cause; and let them say continually, "Let the Lord be magnified, Who has pleasure in the prosperity of His servant"* (Psalm 35:27).

CHAPTER 17

THE ADVANTAGE OF THANKFULNESS

Thankfulness is power. Many have no idea of the power that is available to the thankful. Some live their lives constantly complaining, criticizing, and lamenting how bad things are. There is power in complaining, but not the power you desire.

Having been through a life-and-death battle with cancer, I feel that I have been given a second life. I liken it to a video game in which your character fails and is eliminated, but because you had enough points built up, you get a new character. Not that this was based on points, but I feel I have a new life. This experience has produced in me a thankfulness that I never knew before. I am thankful for waking up, being able to drive my car, being able to teach again, eat out with my wife, and visit with my kids and grandkids. The list is endless. I am simply thankful for everything. I enjoy every day, and if I ever feel the urge to complain, I stop and remember—life is a gift, it is an opportunity to be a blessing, and no matter what happens, I can always be thankful! It has changed my approach to everything.

Thankful people are happy people. They recognize God as their Source. They are grateful for every day and thankful in the midst of any circumstance. They have seen something that many have not. They understand the source of all goodness is God. They are using the advantage of spiritual eyes to see the blessings that are all around. They are not intimidated by bad news. True thankfulness has established God on the throne of their lives.

Thankfulness is the advantage that leads to increase and blessing!

> *Let the peoples praise You, O God; Let all the peoples praise You. Then the earth shall yield her increase; God, our own God, shall bless us* (Psalm 67:5-6).

When you are thankful, you are giving God praise. You are acknowledging His goodness in your life. The memories you allow in your mind are memories of God's blessings.

You refuse to live in the negative events of the past. You are free to see the future through the eyes of thankfulness.

According to Psalm 67 (above), the promise of such thankfulness is increase and blessing. One of the secrets of increase in life is thankfulness. It is a powerful advantage to those who understand it.

Thankfulness is the door into the presence of God.

Enter into His gates with thanksgiving, and into His courts with praise. Be thankful to Him, and bless His name (Psalm 100:4).

Many miss His presence because they never recognize His goodness. Too often we approach God from a place of misery, not thankfulness. Perhaps you feel that there is nothing to be thankful for, but that attitude is stealing your advantage. It is a thankful heart that unlocks the resources of God to change your circumstances.

For the Lord is good; His mercy is everlasting, and His truth endures to all generations (Psalm 100:5).

Be thankful that you wake up in the morning. Be thankful that you have a roof over your head. Be thankful that you have food to eat. Be thankful for your health, even in the midst of health challenges. Healing flows from a thankful heart.

> *Bless the Lord, O my soul; and all that is within me, bless His holy name! Bless the Lord, O my soul, and forget not all His benefits: who forgives all your iniquities, who heals all your diseases* (Psalm 103:1-3).

Even if you struggle to find anything good that has happened in your life, be thankful that God loves you and has forgiven you! Start with that. The more you understand the advantage of thankfulness, the more quickly you will be delivered from your challenges and step into the life God desires for you.

> *Who redeems your life from destruction, who crowns you with lovingkindness and tender mercies* (Psalm 103:4).

What you are thankful for will increase in your life.

> *May the Lord give you increase more and more, you and your children. ...But we will bless the Lord from this time forth and forevermore. Praise the Lord!* (Psalm 115:14, 18).

God is a God of increase, and thankfulness is the environment for His increase.

Thankfulness is a powerful advantage for those who recognize the goodness of God. Focusing on His goodness releases more of that goodness continually.

> *Blessed be the Lord, who daily loads us with benefits, the God of our salvation!* (Psalm 68:19)

A complaining, ungrateful heart will block the blessings of God. The critic loses the advantage. Some find fault with everything. They criticize their church, their pastor, the music, even the carpet and decorations. They sacrifice the presence of God and instead do the work of the "accuser of the brethren." They have lost the advantage.

> *Because, although they knew God, they did not glorify Him as God, nor were thankful, but became futile in their thoughts, and their foolish hearts were darkened* (Romans 1:21).

Unthankfulness will lead to a darkened heart. It will lead to a futile mind. Unthankfulness does not lead to life.

Unthankful people constantly replay their complaints and losses, while thankful people pre-play their victories. They understand that God is for them and that Jesus came to give abundant life to those who believe. Thankful people are believers. The unthankful are in unbelief. Their lives are dictated by circumstances, not by the revelation of God's goodness.

> *In everything give thanks; for this is the will of God in Christ Jesus for you* (1 Thessalonians 5:18).

Thankfulness is a choice, but it is a choice that unlocks a tremendous advantage for the thankful. Thankfulness establishes you in His peace. Thankfulness will activate faith. Thankfulness will deliver you from discouragement and depression.

> *Anxiety in the heart of man causes depression, but a good word makes it glad* (Proverbs 12:25).

That good word could come from your own mouth! The sacrifice of praise and thanksgiving is the key that can free you from anxiety and depression.

> *Therefore by Him let us continually offer the sacrifice of praise to God, that is, the fruit of our lips, giving thanks to His name* (Hebrews 13:15).

Thankfulness uses the power of words to establish the heart and change the circumstances. Thankfulness is faith in action! Thankfulness is a powerful advantage to the believer. Choose to be thankful. Make it a habit in your life. Rather than complaining, look for the good. Give your heart a chance to be filled with His goodness. You'll soon see the clouds lift and the blessings of God break through.

And let the peace of God rule in your hearts, to which also you were called in one body; and be thankful (Colossians 3:15).

CHAPTER 18

THE ADVANTAGE OF FAITH

As I mentioned earlier in this book, my study and growing revelation of God's goodness has done more to activate my faith than my many hours and years of studying the subject of faith. It finally dawned on me that faith is not a subject as much as it is a result of knowing God and walking with Him. In fact, it is a "fruit" of the Spirit.

> *But the fruit of the Spirit is love, joy, peace, long-suffering, gentleness, goodness, faith, meekness, temperance: against such there is no law* (Galatians 5:22-23 KJV).

In the Greek the word is "faith, assurance, belief." It is the same word translated as *faith* throughout the New Testament. I believe the King James Version is a better rendering than the word *faithfulness* found in many other versions. While faithfulness is a characteristic of the faith within us, faith itself is a fruit of the Spirit. In other words, faith is a result of walking in the Spirit and in fellowship with God.

The advantage of faith can't be measured. It is absolute trust in the One who has covenanted to live in you, bless you, and give you His life.

When we understand that faith is the nature of the Spirit of God, we will value our fellowship with Him, knowing that the more we know Him, the more we will trust Him, and the more that trust will have access to His blessings (advantages).

The expression of your faith can change dramatically from day to day, depending upon how your heart relates to God's Word and Spirit. It is with the heart man believes (Romans 10:10). Living by faith is living by the Word of God that is alive in your heart in every circumstance. When we approach faith as a subject like math or science, I believe we lose the true essence of what faith is. In its purest form, faith is a manifestation of our fellowship with the Source of faith.

Looking unto Jesus, the author and finisher of our faith (Hebrews 12:2).

For that reason, Jesus exhorted that "*Man shall not live by bread alone, but by every word that proceeds from the mouth of God*" (Matthew 4:4). The words that proceed from God's mouth and find the good soil of our hearts produce the fruit of faith we must live by. God's life in us flows from His words living in us, as do health, joy, peace, prosperity, and vision for the future. The advantage is very real! The "natural man" (and even the believer who lives from his or her own strength) is left with a life of frustration and questions.

> *But the natural man does not receive the things of the Spirit of God, for they are foolishness to him; nor can he know them, because they are spiritually discerned* (1 Corinthians 2:14).

Our advantage is that we are born again and spiritual. And the fruit, or result, of this spiritual union is faith. Jesus said:

> *If you can believe, all things are possible to him who believes* (Mark 9:23).

"All things are possible to him who believes!" Is that not an advantage? The only qualifier is believing—faith. And as we abide in Him, faith is a result.

If you abide in Me, and My words abide in you, you will ask what you desire, and it shall be done for you (John 15:7).

When a child asks something of a parent, it is in the parent's heart to grant the request. While not every request can be granted in this natural world, our heavenly Father has promised to grant what we desire. How? Because we know Him and trust Him. It is called faith. And why would He grant our desires?

By this My Father is glorified, that you bear much fruit; so you will be My disciples (John 15:8).

Our faith glorifies God! The more we believe and receive from Him, the more the world will see how good God is. Your faith not only is an advantage in your own life, but a blessing to those around you. When you trust God, the fruit of that trust reveals Him to others. That is an advantage that the lost don't have.

Faith is not a stagnant, one-time event that marks our new birth. Faith is not a creed or doctrine. Faith is not mental. Faith is spiritual. It is a fruit of the Holy Spirit. It is called "the spirit of faith."

*And since we have the same **spirit of faith**, according to what is written, "I believed and therefore I spoke," we also believe and therefore speak* (2 Corinthians 4:13).

What is written are words of spirit and life!

It is the Spirit who gives life; the flesh profits nothing. The words that I speak to you are spirit, and they are life (John 6:63).

We have come full circle back to the incredible potential of words. The words of faith are spiritual words that release the very Spirit of God. The fruit of faith produces the fruit of words, and the words carry the nature and purposes of God. Can you see the awesome advantage that God's children have?

FAITH AND LOVE

When we walk in love, we demonstrate the nature of God to others. When we walk in faith, we demonstrate His will. The kind of faith that pleases God works by love!

For in Christ Jesus neither circumcision nor uncircumcision avails anything, but faith working through love (Galatians 5:6).

Paul is saying that religious works (circumcision, law-keeping) or the lack of religious works is not proof of our walk with God, but rather it is our faith which is an outflow of God's love. Love is the environment for true faith. Paul declared:

> *And though I have all faith, so that I could remove mountains, but have not love, I am nothing* (1 Corinthians 13:2).

Even those who profess great faith but have no love for others aren't really walking in God's faith.

When we fellowship with the Father (who is love), we enter the realm of His faith (fruit) flowing through us, which pleases Him. True faith is an expression of the love of God.

Consider some examples. The centurion, a Roman with no covenant or promises, approached Jesus on behalf of his servant.

> *And a certain centurion's servant, who was dear to him, was sick and ready to die* (Luke 7:2).

His servant was "dear to him." There was love for this dying servant. While the centurion had no covenant advantage, and really nothing to commend him to Jesus, nevertheless, his love for his servant compelled him to humble himself and ask that Jesus just speak a word, and his servant would be healed. Notice Jesus' reply.

> *When Jesus heard these things, He marveled at him, and turned around and said to the crowd that followed Him, "I say to you, I have not found such great faith, not even in Israel!"* (Luke 7:9)

The centurion's minimal interaction with Jesus coupled with his love for his servant was all the advantage he needed. Jesus called it "great faith." The "disadvantage" of being a Roman soldier with no covenant and no promises did not hinder a miracle healing due to his love for his servant and his brief conversation with Jesus.

We can see this kind of faith in the stories of Jairus and his dying daughter in Matthew 5:21-45 and the story of the Canaanite woman and her demon-possessed daughter in Matthew 15:22-28. The love of both parents for their children provoked a faith that recognized the goodness of Jesus and His authority. *Faith works by love*, and the love of a parent released faith in the love of Jesus, who in turn released His faith and healed both children. People with seemingly no advantage suddenly were advantaged by faith, which worked by love!

For God so loved the world, that He gave His only begotten Son, that whoever believes in Him shall not perish, but have eternal life (John 3:16 NASB).

God's love was given to the world through Jesus so that men could have faith in Him. Love gives and love forgives. When we walk in love, we also give and forgive. The love of God motivates us to reach the world so that others can believe and receive that love.

For whatever is born of God overcomes the world. And this is the victory that has overcome the world—our faith (1 John 5:4).

Faith overcomes the world! But this is not a faith we can work up outside of our fellowship with the Father who loves us and gave Himself for us. We cannot walk in faith independent from the loving Source of faith.

Faith overcomes the corruption of the world so that His love can be demonstrated to the lost. Faith is the currency of heaven. It is His divine method for reaching the world with His love and establishing His will. Love wants to heal. Faith makes that happen. Love wants to deliver. Faith brings deliverance. Love wants to save. Faith receives salvation.

Therefore be imitators of God as dear children. And walk in love, as Christ also has loved us and given Himself for us (Ephesians 5:1-2).

Those with true faith are those who know the love of God. If your faith seems weak, check your revelation of God's love for you and for the world. Faith will not waste time judging, criticizing, and complaining. That is the language of the "accuser." Faith will seek to bless, forgive, lift up, encourage, and bring healing to others because the love of God has been shed abroad in our hearts by the Holy Spirit, and the fruit of the Spirit is faith!

Now hope does not disappoint, because the love of God has been poured out in our hearts by the Holy Spirit who was given to us (Romans 5:5).

But the fruit of the Spirit is love...faith (Galatians 5:22 KJV).

CHAPTER 19

THE ADVANTAGE OF UNBELIEF

No doubt that title will stir some questions. How could unbelief possibly be an advantage? The unbelieving miss out on the abundant blessings of God.

One day as I was reading in the Gospel of Mark, I came across the story of Jesus ministering in His own hometown.

Now He could do no mighty work there, except that He laid His hands on a few sick people and healed them. And He marveled because of their unbelief. Then He went about the villages in a circuit, teaching (Mark 6:5-6).

I sensed the Spirit speak to me and say, "If unbelief can stop the power of God, could it not also stop the power of the enemy?" As I meditated on this, I realized that we all have a choice as to what we believe or choose to not believe. Everyone reading this book believes something. Some beliefs are firmly rooted in the heart, and some are opinions subject to change.

Being told to get my affairs in order and that I was going to die was a surreal moment. I can remember the supernatural peace that came over me and I felt the Spirit quicken me that I would not die from this large, cancerous tumor. I chose to not believe the words of the doctor. In a sense, I was in unbelief—unbelief in the negative, and in faith for the positive.

Too often we believe every piece of bad news that we are exposed to. If we go to the Lord, it is often in a state of panic or fear. Not only have we believed the negative report, but we also begin to struggle with our faith in God. Why doesn't He do something? Where is God when you need Him?

Why does our faith in bad news seem to be stronger than our faith in the Good News? I thank God that my relationship with Him, my foundation in the Word, and my revelation of His goodness were all barriers against the "bad news." *My unbelief in bad news was strong!* It's not that the tumor wasn't real or that my body wasn't in trouble. It's just that my faith in God simultaneously put me in a place of powerful unbelief in the negative report.

*Surely he will never be shaken; the righteous will be in everlasting remembrance. **He will not be afraid of evil tidings;** his heart is steadfast, trusting in the Lord. His heart is established; he will not be afraid, until he sees his desire upon his enemies* (Psalm 112:6-8).

When the voices around you declare the impossibility of your circumstances, it is good to have unbelief in those voices. Why would we give more attention to the voices of doubt than to the promises of God? Don't believe the fear. Don't believe the negativity. Don't believe that something is impossible. Stay in unbelief in that which is temporal. It is much easier to believe in the provision and grace of God if you start by refusing to believe that which comes to steal, kill, and destroy.

You already believe something. Faith is not something that is worked up. Faith and unbelief both flow from the voices we hear (spiritual or natural), that which feeds us spiritually or emotionally, and that which we value. Those who give their time to the voices of the world often struggle with believing the Word of God. Those who give their time to fellowshipping with God in His Word will find it much easier to ignore the voices of the world. They will not be afraid of evil tidings (see Psalm 112:6-8 above).

Choose unbelief in sickness, poverty, fear, and depression. You have the advantage! You get to choose what you will believe and what you will reject. Choose the promises of God. Reject the voice of the enemy and the doubts of the world. Don't waste your advantage!

CHAPTER 20

SO MANY ADVANTAGES!

When we begin to understand how God has blessed us with every blessing, it is easy to recognize those blessings (advantages) in everyday life. Believers are never at a disadvantage. We have the Name of Jesus, the most powerful Name there is! We can declare His Name, proclaim His Name, and pray in His Name.

> *That at the name of Jesus every knee should bow, of those in heaven, and of those on earth, and of those under the earth* (Philippians 2:10).

There is no power or name that is greater than the Name of Jesus! When we speak that Name in faith, the spiritual world and the physical world come to attention.

> *Then Peter said, "Silver and gold I do not have, but what I do have I give you: In the name of Jesus Christ of Nazareth, rise up and walk"* (Acts 3:6).

There is power in the Name of Jesus! His Name gives us the advantage in every situation.

We have the Holy Spirit living within.

> *But if the Spirit of Him who raised Jesus from the dead dwells in you, He who raised Christ from the dead will also give life to your mortal bodies through His Spirit who dwells in you* (Romans 8:11).

What a powerful verse! We who have the Spirit of God living within are receiving continual "life" in our bodies. We are graced and strengthened for the abundant life. We have the advantage!

We have the better covenant established on better promises.

> *But now He has obtained a more excellent ministry, inasmuch as He is also Mediator of a better covenant, which was established on better promises* (Hebrews 8:6).

We are not under a covenant of blessings and curses based on behavior. We are under a covenant of blessings based on Jesus' finished work on the cross, His resurrection from the dead, and His gift of righteousness to all who believe. We need not look to Job for our understanding of the new creation. We now look unto Jesus!

> *Looking unto Jesus, the author and finisher of our faith, who for the joy that was set before Him endured the cross, despising the shame, and has sat down at the right hand of the throne of God* (Hebrews 12:2).

We have the Word of God, which is alive with the life of God.

> *For the word of God is living and powerful, and sharper than any two-edged sword, piercing even to the division of soul and spirit, and of joints and marrow, and is a discerner of the thoughts and intents of the heart* (Hebrews 4:12).

This living Word was sent to heal and deliver us.

> *He sent His word and healed them, and delivered them from their destructions* (Psalm 107:20).

His Word sustains us, empowers us, reveals Him to us, and activates faith in us.

As for God, His way is perfect; the word of the Lord is proven; He is a shield to all who trust in Him (Psalm 18:30).

So then faith comes by hearing, and hearing by the word of God (Romans 10:17).

We have our new identity in Christ.

Therefore, if anyone is in Christ, he is a new creation; old things have passed away; behold, all things have become new (2 Corinthians 5:17).

Unbelievers are still locked in the "old things" of this fallen world, but believers have moved into the world of Spirit and Life. We have the advantage if we would recognize it and believe it.

We have the armor of God.

Therefore take up the whole armor of God, that you may be able to withstand in the evil day, and having done all, to stand (Ephesians 6:13).

God's grace has given us the gift of righteousness, the blessing of the gospel, faith, salvation, and the Word of God which is the sword of the Spirit. Can you see that as a child of God, you have so many advantages that there is no reason to be defeated, depressed, and overwhelmed with life? God has graced us with every blessing.

> *Blessed be the God and Father of our Lord Jesus Christ, who has blessed us with every spiritual blessing in the heavenly places in Christ* (Ephesians 1:3).

We have His authority.

> *Behold, I give you the authority to trample on serpents and scorpions, and over all the power of the enemy, and nothing shall by any means hurt you* (Luke 10:19).

The authority that was delegated to the disciples is now inherent in believers. He who has *all* authority in heaven and in earth now lives in us! We no longer have a spirit of fear.

> *For God has not given us a spirit of fear, but of power and of love and of a sound mind* (2 Timothy 1:7).

We have His faith. By the Spirit that lives in us we have the nature of God, and His nature includes His faith!

Above all, taking the shield of faith with which you will be able to quench all the fiery darts of the wicked one (Ephesians 6:16).

*But the fruit of the Spirit is love, joy, peace, long-suffering, gentleness, goodness, **faith*** (Galatians 5:22 KJV).

Can the faith of God fail? We were created to hear God, believe God, and do the works of God!

Most assuredly, I say to you, he who believes in Me, the works that I do he will do also; and greater works than these he will do, because I go to My Father (John 14:12).

We have His forgiveness and His righteousness.

I write unto you, little children, because your sins are forgiven you for his name's sake (1 John 2:12 KJV).

Many have understood forgiveness, but haven't fully grasped the power of righteousness that has been given to those who believe.

For if by one man's offence death reigned by one; much more they which receive abundance of grace and of the gift of righteousness shall reign in life by one, Jesus Christ (Romans 5:17 KJV).

It is clear that believers are meant to "reign in life" and not be perpetual victims. The promises of the New Covenant were made during Roman occupation and oppression. That didn't stop Jesus and the other New Testament writers from declaring God's possibilities for His people! All things are possible to those who believe (see Mark 9:23).

We have His peace.

Peace I leave with you, My peace I give to you; not as the world gives do I give to you. Let not your heart be troubled, neither let it be afraid (John 14:27).

While others strive for a circumstantial peace in their own strength, believers have a peace that passes understanding that lives within. In spite of the circumstances, believers can walk in peace and know that they are fully equipped to navigate the challenges of this life. His peace is our strength! We have the advantage!

The Lord will give strength to His people; the Lord will bless His people with peace (Psalm 29:11).

We have His joy.

These things I have spoken to you, that My joy may remain in you, and that your joy may be full (John 15:11).

While the world searches for temporary happiness, we have the joy of the Lord that is our strength!

Whom having not seen you love. Though now you do not see Him, yet believing, you rejoice with joy inexpressible and full of glory (1 Peter 1:8).

The joy of a believer is a fruit of the Spirit and does not depend on circumstances. Paul and Silas were joyful and singing praises in prison (see Acts 16:25-26)! When we fail to access His peace and joy, we lose the advantage and the potential for victory.

We have His love shed abroad in our hearts!

Now hope does not disappoint, because the love of God has been poured out in our hearts by the Holy Spirit who was given to us (Romans 5:5).

God, who is love, now lives inside of you! We are not limited to the roller coaster of human "love" and emotions that come and go. We have the spiritual nature of God Himself within, and we are now able to love others in spite of their actions. We see with a different perspective. We understand the common needs and hurts that people live with, and we have something to give. We aren't looking for what we can get from others or how we can get even with those who have hurt us. Rather, we can now draw from God's love and minister to those who are hurting and may not know why.

> *Beloved, let us love one another, for love is of God; and everyone who loves is born of God and knows God. ...Beloved, if God so loved us, we also ought to love one another* (1 John 4:7, 11).

The advantage of God's love cannot be measured. We don't have to live as natural men and women. We don't have to be driven by human emotions, hurts, and failures. As believers, we have the advantages in life. We can overcome!

With all of these advantages, how could we ever feel helpless? Shouldn't we be more than conquerors instead of complaining victims?

CHAPTER 21

YOU ALWAYS HAVE THE ADVANTAGE IN CHRIST

My purpose in writing this book is to encourage believers to recognize the tremendous advantages we have as born-again believers and to take advantage of the advantages in order to live the abundant life Jesus came to give us.

> *The thief does not come except to steal, and to kill, and to destroy. I have come that they may have life, and that they may have it more abundantly* (John 10:10).

The lives of far too many Christians reflect more the work of the thief than the blessing of God. Our advantages haven't been taught, or sadly, may have been taught *against* in some circles. The full blessing of the gospel is lost in a religious world of clichés, guilt, unbelief, and denial.

*But I know that when I come to you, I shall come in the **fullness of the blessing of the gospel of Christ*** (Romans 15:29).

You are never at a disadvantage in Christ. You always have the advantage in every situation. While others are limited to the corruption of darkness, you have unlimited access to God's Kingdom provision. While others are dominated by the "god of this world," you are filled with the Greater One! While others are in bondage to fear, you are filled with the Spirit of God, love, power, and the mind of Christ.

While others see limitations and defeat, you see victory and abundance. While others speak fear, doubt, and unbelief, you speak words of life and faith. While others feel abandoned and helpless, you know that you have God's favor and that He will never leave you nor forsake you!

Let your conduct be without covetousness; be content with such things as you have. For He Himself has said, "I will never leave you nor forsake you" (Hebrews 13:5).

This is the renewing of the mind that transforms the believer from victim to victor!

And do not be conformed to this world, but be transformed by the renewing of your mind, that you may prove what is that good and acceptable and perfect will of God (Romans 12:2).

Choose today to walk in newness of life! Let your heart be filled with the revelation of the advantages of God's grace and love. You can reign in life if you believe. *You have the advantage!*

ABOUT BARRY BENNETT

A graduate of Christ for the Nations Institute in Dallas, Texas, Barry has served the Lord since 1972. He and his wife, Betty Kay, ministered to Cambodian refugees in Dallas for nearly three years and served as missionaries in Mexico, Guatemala, and Chile for over 12 years. In 2001, they returned to Texas, where Barry served as director and teacher at a Spanish language Bible institute. In 2007, Barry joined Andrew Wommack Ministries, where he has served as Dean of Students and now serves as a Senior Instructor.

From

Barry Bennett

Healing is God's Will!

There's no evidence in the Gospels of sickness having a divine origin or being a blessing in disguise. Jesus never withheld healing from someone who asked. He was always full of compassion to heal the sick.

"...Great multitudes followed Him [Jesus], **and He healed them all"** *(Matt 12:15 NKJV).*

In *He Healed Them All*, author Barry Bennett shares the amazing truth that Jesus still heals every sickness. The grace of God is bigger than any affliction you may be experiencing.

So get your hopes up! It's never too late or too hard! Healing is always God's will.

There is grace today for you to be healed!

Purchase your copy wherever books are sold